FIRE APPLIANCES OF SOUTH WEST ENGLAND

EDDIE BAKER

Published by EB Books,
5 Lordsway Park,
Alconbury,
Huntingdon,
PE28 4BF.

First published 2015

Text© Eddie Baker 2015
Images © as attributed

The moral right of Eddie Baker to be identified as the author of this work has been asserted.

Printed and bound by Printondemand, Peterborough

ISBN: 978-0-9934684-0-7

Front Cover Photos

Top – Somerset Water Tender Ladder (Colin Carter)
Middle Left - Wiltshire Dennis Sabre Water Tender Ladder (Malcolm Thompson)
Middle Right - Dorset Scania Water Tender Ladder (Colin Dunford)
Bottom - Gloucestershire Scania Special Rescue Tender (The Author)

CONTENTS

ABOUT THE AUTHOR

Eddie Baker's father was one of the first volunteers to join the Auxiliary Fire Service (AFS) prior to the Second World War and served in both the AFS and National Fire Service (NFS) through to 1947, when he became a Section Leader (Sub Officer) in charge of a watch at Croydon Airport Fire Service. When the airport closed he became a works fire officer at Croydon B Power Station until his retirement. He also served as treasurer for the Croydon area of the Fire Brigades Union (FBU) for many years. As a child Eddie spent many hours at the airport fire station and travelling with his father around Croydon's fire stations collecting FBU subscriptions. Therefore it was inevitable that he would have a lifelong interest in the fire service.

Eddie joined the fire service in 1960 when he enrolled in the Croydon Auxiliary Fire Service. He was promoted through the ranks to Sub Officer prior to the time of amalgamation with the London Fire Brigade in 1965. He continued to serve in the AFS until it disbanded in 1968. By 1970 Eddie had moved home and joined the Cambridgeshire and Isle of Ely Fire Brigade and was initially stationed at Gamlingay Fire Station. After local government re-organisation in 1974 he served with the Cambridgeshire Fire and Rescue Service and transferred to St. Neots Fire Station in 1977 before retiring in 1995 as a Leading Fire-fighter.

Married to Ann they have a son Mark, a daughter Lisa and three granddaughters and four great-grandchildren. Since his retirement Eddie has continued his interest in the Fire Service and this is his sixth book on the subject. He has also written a number of articles which have been published in Fire Service related magazines. Eddie also gives talks to local groups on the history of the UK Fire Service.

Also by Eddie Baker:

On The Run: A History of Croydon Fire Brigade
A History of Firefighting in Cambridgeshire
Fire Appliances of Eastern England
Airfield Firefighting in Eastern England
Industrial Firefighting in Eastern England

ACKNOWLEDGEMENTS

Many old friends and some new ones have assisted with this book. Gary Chapman deserves a special mention for the inspiration to write this book and for the use of his photographic collection. Other photographs have come from the collections of Colin Carter, Ken Davis, Colin Dunford, Graham Eglen, the late Mike Lawmon, the late Mike Williams and the late Roy Yeoman. Many others, too numerous to individually acknowledge here, have also supplied photographs; however their names appear in the relevant captions. There is also a number of photographs marked 'unknown photographer' and all reasonable efforts have been made to trace these photographers and it is hoped that they can be duly credited in future editions. I must also give thanks to the various Fire and Rescue Services who have assisted with the production of this book.

INTRODUCTION

This book describes the fire appliances that previously operated and currently operate within the local authority Fire and Rescue Services of the South-West of England; namely Avon, Cornwall, Devon & Somerset, Dorset, Gloucestershire, The Isles of Scilly and Wiltshire. As a bonus an additional chapter has been included on the Fire Service College at Moreton in Marsh. The book concentrates on the appliances that have been in use from the time of the Fire Service de-nationalisation in 1948 when the local county brigades were first set up through to the present day. It does of course include some of the vehicles from the pre-war and wartime days which were taken over by the newly formed brigades.

In 1948 when the Fire Service was de-nationalised the South-West was covered by six County Brigades, five City Brigades and one County Borough Brigade. A major problem facing these newly formed brigades was the financial implications of the wartime debt which was crippling local authorities. At the same time commercial chassis production was limited due to lack of raw materials and the initial supply of new appliances was controlled by the Home Office who placed block orders with manufacturers and supplied vehicles to individual brigades on a priority basis. As a consequent manufacturers and brigade workshops showed great ingenuity in converting, or even completely rebuilding wartime appliances into new roles until the early 1950s when it became possible for brigades to place their own orders. At this time the demand for new appliances far exceeded the capabilities of the pre-war manufacturers such as Dennis Brothers, Leyland and Merryweather & Sons. Consequently many body building companies entered the market, building on commercial chassis; mainly Bedford and Commer. Many of these companies ceased production of fire appliances by the mid 1950s once the initial log-jam of orders was completed.

The number of brigades has reduced due to local government mergers and the book describes the appliances of the constituent brigades that were in existence before these mergers as well as those of the current Fire and Rescue Services. These mergers resulted in the formation of larger vehicle fleets and the introduction of a greater degree of standardisation, in particular with pumping appliances. This contrasts to the smaller brigades that previously existed, where local risks and needs provided for more specialisation and variation in the fleets. The appliances featured in the following chapters include examples of the standard types commonly seen and some of the more unusual vehicles that operated since the formation of the local authorities in 1948.

Since the early 1970s pumping appliances have been introduced with inter-changeable roles and can be in the form of either a Water Tender or a Water Tender Ladder dependent on the equipment and ladders carried. Latterly the terminology Rescue Pump has also been introduced by some Fire and Rescue Services. For the purposes of this book I have used the term Water Tender when describing appliances purchased although, of course, they can be used for all three variants.

Following the disastrous events in New York on the 9th September 2001 the UK Government implemented a programme to ensure that the UK's Fire and Rescue Services could cope with major chemical, nuclear, biological and terrorist threats. The programme was established by the Office of the Deputy Prime Minister (ODPM) which was succeeded by the Department for Communities and Local Government. The vehicles include Incident Response Units, Prime Movers, High Volume Pumping Units, Urban Search and Research Units, Mass Decontamination Disrobe and Re-Robe Units and Detection Identification and Monitoring Units. The role of each vehicle is dealt with in a separate chapter along with the allocations within each Fire and Rescue Service.

CHAPTER 1
AVON

The County of Avon was formed on 1ˢᵗ April 1974 comprising the City of Bristol, the City of Bath, parts of Somerset and parts of Gloucestershire. The County of Avon was abolished in 1996 and replaced with four smaller unitary authorities; Bristol City Council, Bath and North East Somerset District Council, North Somerset District Council and South Gloucestershire District Council. A combined fire authority was formed to cover the same area. To better reflect the changing role of fire brigades the Fire and Rescue Services Act of 2004 was passed leading Avon Fire Brigade to change its name to Avon Fire & Rescue Service.

City of Bath Fire Brigade 1948-1974

The new City of Bath Fire Brigade was created on the 1ˢᵗ April 1948 with the strength of a Chief Fire Officer, a Deputy Chief Fire Officer (ADO rank), two Sub Officers, four Leading Firemen and thirty-six Firemen. There was also a retained complement of one Sub Officer, two Leading Firemen and nine Firemen. There were only two fire appliances remaining from the pre-war fleet; a 1940 Albion Pump Escape and a 1936 Albion Turntable Ladder. The remainder were ex-NFS vehicles including an Austin K4 Heavy Unit, an Austin K2 Auxiliary Towing Vehicle (ATV) and Trailer Pump, a Fordson Water Tender, a Fordson Hose Layer and a Studebaker car operating as a Chimney Van.

Bath Fire Brigade in 1949 –Austin K4 Pump GLE 907, Austin K2 ATV GLR 226, Albion Pump Escape GL 7566 and Albion/Merryweather Turntable Ladder GL 4110 (Unknown photographer)

Appliances known to have served with City of Bath Fire Brigade

Built	Type	Chassis	Body	Reg. No.
1936	Turntable Ladder	Albion	Merryweather 100ft	GL 4110
1940	Chimney Van	Studebaker		GL4400
1940	Pump Escape	Albion		GL 7566
1941	Hose Layer	Fordson 7v		GGN 630
1942	Pump (1)	Austin K4		GLE 907
1942	Water Tender	Fordson 7v		GLW 124
1942	ATV	Austin K2		GGX 100
1942	ATV	Austin K2		GLR 226
1942	ATV	Austin K2		GYR 851
1942	Hosereel Tender (2)	Austin K2		GLR 648
1952	Water Tender	Bedford S	Miles	DFB 499
1953	Pump Escape	Dennis F12		DFB 999
1956	Turntable Ladder	AEC Regent	Merryweather 100ft	GFB 712
1957	L4P	Land Rover 88	Carmichael	HFB 821
1960	Dual Purpose (3)	Bedford C5Z	Hampshire Car Bodies	KGL 430
1961	Rescue Tender (4)	Land Rover	Carmichael	MFB 471
1963	Pump Escape	Bedford TKEL		NGL 664
1964	Hose Layer (5)	Commer KC40		AFB 638B
1967	Pump Escape	Dennis F106		FFB 109F
1967	Turntable Ladder	AEC Mercury	Merryweather 100ft	EGL 678F
1969	Water Tender	Dennis F108		GGL 131G
1969	Rescue Boat	C-Craft		
1972	Rescue Tender	Land Rover FC101	Carmichael	NGL 999L

(1)   Former NFS Heavy Unit
(2)   Former NFS ATV purchased from Dorset Fire Brigade in 1958
(3)   When used as a Pump Escape it only carried 200 gallons of water
(4)   Converted to Lighting Unit in 1973
(5)   Later converted to a Canteen Van by Longwell Green

The first new appliance delivered was a Bedford Water Tender built by Alfred Miles which arrived in November 1952 followed in July 1953 by a Dennis F12 Pump Escape. These new appliances allowed the disposal of the Studebaker car, with the Fordson Water Tender being retained as a reserve appliance and the Austin Heavy Unit being transferred to the reformed Auxiliary Fire Service. By the mid 1950s the pre-war Turntable Ladder was showing signs of deterioration although the ladders were still in good condition. The vehicle was returned to Merryweathers and the ladders overhauled and remounted on a new AEC Regent chassis in 1956. While the work was being carried out Bristol Fire Brigade loaned a Turntable Ladder to Bath. Two more appliances were purchased in the 1950s; a Land Rover L4P in 1957 and a second-hand Hosereel Tender based on an ex-NFS ATV which came from Dorset Fire Brigade in 1958.

1960 saw a Dual Purpose appliance purchased, which could be used as either a Pump Escape or a Water Tender built by Hampshire Car Bodies (HCB) on a Bedford chassis. An innovative appliance was designed by the brigade and delivered in 1961. This was a Rescue Tender based on a long-wheel base Land Rover and built by Carmichaels of Worcester. Bath was the first brigade in the country to place this type of appliance on the road. A second Pump Escape was placed on the run in 1963 when HCB supplied a Bedford TK based appliance. The wartime Hose Layer was replaced in 1964 with a new vehicle utilising a Commer 'Walkthru' van

Bath Fire Brigade's first new appliance was this 1952 Bedford
'S' type Water Tender reg. no. DFB 499 built by Alfred Miles
(The Wardell Collection)

1956 AEC Regent Turntable Ladder reg. no. GFB 712 fitted
with the pre-war Merryweather 100 feet ladders
(Unknown photographer)

1967 AEC Mercury Turntable Ladder reg. no. EGL 678F fitted
with Merryweather 100 feet ladders
(photo – Mike Lawmon)

The 1973 Land Rover Forward Control Rescue Tender reg. no.
NGL 999L with Carmichael bodywork (Unknown photographer)

The late 1960s saw the completion of the planned replacement of the fleet with the purchase of three new appliances; a Dennis F106 Pump Escape and an AEC Mercury/Merryweather Turntable Ladder both in 1967 and a Dennis F108 Water Tender in 1969. Also in 1969 a Rescue Boat was supplied which was towed by the Land Rover Rescue Tender.

The last appliance ordered by Bath Fire Brigade was a replacement for the Rescue Tender. Again a Land Rover vehicle was chosen but this time a forward control model built by Carmichaels.

Bristol Fire Brigade 1948-1974

Bristol Fire Brigade was reformed in 1948 with a complement of 235 operational firefighters and six fire stations., Appliances taken over from the National Fire Service included six Pump Escapes, seven Pumps, three Water Tenders, three Turntable Ladders, two Foam Tenders, two Hose Layers, an Emergency Tender, a Salvage Tender, a Breathing Apparatus Tender, a Canteen Van and two Fireboats; the *Pyronaut* in the City Docks and the *Endes Gane* based in Avonmouth.

Appliances known to have been taken over by Bristol Fire Brigade in 1948

Built	Type	Chassis	Body	Reg. No.
1931	Pump Escape	Leyland		HY 1801
1932	Pump Escape	Leyland FT1		HY 4979
1933	Pump Escape	Leyland FT1		HY 9756
1933	Fireboat	Charles Hill		*Pyronaut*
1936	Fireboat	Charles Hill		*Endres Gane*
1936	Turntable Ladder	Leyland	Merryweather 100ft	CAE 965
1936	Pump	Leyland Cub FK6		CHW 353
1937	Pump Escape	Leyland		DHY 496
1938	Turntable Ladder	Albion FE6	Merryweather 100ft	FHT 674
1940	Escape Carrier	Fordson 7v		GGK 113
1941	Pump	Leyland		HHT 183
1942	Heavy Unit	Bedford		FYH 418
1942	ATV	Austin K2		GGX 256
1942	Heavy Unit	Fordson 7v		GJJ 129
1942	ATV	Austin K2		GLC 653
1942	ATV	Austin K2		GLC 751

Built	Type	Chassis	Body	Reg. No.
1942	Salvage Tender	Austin K2		GLC 780
1942	ATV	Austin K2		GLE 214
1942	Foam Tender	Austin K2		GLE 900
1942	Water Tender A (1)	Austin K4		
1943	Turntable Ladder	Dennis	Merryweather 100ft	GLW 424
1943	Emergency Tender	Bedford		GLY 312
1943	Escape Carrier	Austin K4		GXA 720
1944	Water Tender A (1)	Dodge		

(1)   Former Mobile Dam Unit

Appliances were allocated to stations as follows:-

Station 1	Bridewell Street	Pump Escape, 2 Pumps, Turntable Ladder, Emergency Tender, Salvage Tender, Breathing Apparatus Tender, Hose Layer, Canteen Van, Fireboat
Station 2	Stoke Hill	Pump Escape, Water Tender
Station 3	Avonmouth	2 Pumps, Foam Tender, Fireboat
Station 4	Brislington	Pump Escape, Water Tender, Hose Layer
Station 5	Ashton Drive	Pump Escape, Pump, Turntable Ladder
Station 6	Fishponds	Pump Escape, Pump, Water Tender, Turntable Ladder, Foam Tender
	Reserve	Pump Escape, Pump

1937 Leyland FT3A Pump Escape reg. no. DHY 496 (Unknown photographer)

1940 Leyland TLM2 Turntable Ladder reg. no. GHW 415 (Unknown photographer)

Another Leyland appliance was this 1942 F7T1 Pump reg. no. HHT 183 (Unknown photographer)

This 1942 Austin K4 Dam Lorry was converted to a Water Tender and towed a Trailer Pump (Unknown photographer)

The first new appliance delivered, a Dennis F7 Pump Escape, arrived on 22nd February 1950 followed by a Dennis F12 Pump Escape in 1951. Another Dennis appliance was delivered in 1953, this time a Water Tender on the F15 chassis. In 1953 the brigade changed its chassis supplier to Bedford with the purchase of a Water Tender built by HCB. In 1954 Oldland Motor Bodies supplied two appliances, a Water Tender and a Foam Tender both built on the Bedford SH chassis. Oldlands continued to supply appliances to Bristol with a Hose Layer/Salvage Tender in 1955 and three Pump Escapes between 1955 and 1958 again on the Bedford SH chassis. Also in 1955 a Bedford TJ1 Breathing Apparatus Tender was supplied by Hawson and fitted out by Bristol's workshops. 1958 saw the introduction of a new type of fire appliance with the purchase of two Land Rover Light Pumps (L4Ps), one built by Carmichael and one by HCB. The final appliance purchased in the 1950s was a Turntable Ladder delivered in 1959 built by Merryweathers on an AEC chassis with 100 feet ladders.

A Bedford TKEL chassied Emergency Tender was built by HCB in 1961 followed in 1962 by a Hosereel Tender again built by HCB but on a Bedford TJ2 chassis. Three Pumps were delivered between 1962 and 1963; one built by Carmichaels and the other two by HCB all on the Bedford

Bristol's 1950 Dennis F7 Pump Escape reg. no. MHW 800
(The Wardell Collection)

This 1958 Bedford SH Water Tender Escape reg. no. 150 BHW
was built by Oldland Motor Bodies (The Wardell Collection)

1958 Land Rover L4P reg. no. 650 DAE built by HCB
(The Wardell Collection)

1963 Bedford TKEL Pump reg. no. 999 SHY built by HCB
(photo – Bob Smith)

TKEL chassis. There was also a Foam Carrier delivered in 1963, supplied by HCB again on a Bedford TKEL chassis. Two appliances were delivered in 1965; an Austin Gypsy Rescue Tender and a Dennis F34 Water Tender, the first Dennis for twelve years. No more new major pumping appliances were purchased between 1965 and 1969 although a second-hand 1951 Leyland Comet Pump Escape was bought from Warwickshire Fire Brigade as a temporary measure until sold in 1970. In 1966 HCB-Angus (HCB-A) supplied a Karrier VAC Foam Tender and a Land Rover Hosereel Tender. Also in 1966 the brigade's two Fireboats were dry-docked for examination and a major refit was carried out on the *Pyronaut* but major deterioration to the hull of the *Endres Gane* was such that it was uneconomical to repair. Consequently a new Fireboat the *Aquanaut* was ordered from the Thames Launch Co. of Twickenham and delivered in 1969. Meanwhile an ERF based Hydraulic Platform fitted with Simon 65 feet booms and built by HCB-A was purchased in 1967. A steady replacement program of appliances had occurred but it was not until 1968 that the last of the pre-war vehicles was withdrawn when the 1942 Salvage Tender was replaced by a purpose built appliance supplied on a Bedford TJ1 chassis by Hawson. Also in 1968 a Land Rover Rescue Tender built by Carmichaels and an AEC Turntable Ladder with 100 feet Merryweather ladders were delivered. The final appliances purchased in the 1960s were two ERF 84PF Water Tender Escapes built by HCB-A in 1969.

A new appliance delivered in 1970 was a Hi-Expansion Foam Unit converted from a Bedford CF350 van by the brigade's workshops. Two Hosereel Tenders built on the Land Rover 109 chassis by HCB-A were also delivered in 1970. Between 1970 and 1973 the replacement program was accelerated and eight more appliances were delivered for use as either Water Tender Escapes or Water Tenders. Four were built by HCB-A on the ERF 84PF chassis, three on the Dodge K850 chassis again built by HCB-A and the final one built by Jennings on a Dodge K1113 chassis. Two 'specials' were supplied in 1971; a Chemical Incident Unit built by Taylors on a Bedford TKB chassis and a Foam Tender built by Carmichaels on a Dodge K1050 chassis. Oldland Motor Bodies who had supplied pumping appliances in the 1950s re-appeared on the scene in 1972 supplying a Breathing Apparatus Tender/Control Unit and a Hose Layer both on the Bedford TKC chassis. By the early 1970s Simon Engineering had introduced the 85 feet Hydraulic Platform and Bristol Fire Brigade ordered one in 1973 built on the Dodge K1050 chassis by HCB-A.

1971 Bedford TKB Chemical Incident Unit reg. no. BHW 486J built by Taylors (Bob Smith)

1972 ERF 84PF Water Tender Ladder reg. no. DAE 621K built by HCB-A (Bob Smith)

1972 Dodge K1113 Water Tender Escape reg. no. HAE 418K built by Jennings (Unknown photographer)

1972 Bedford TKC Breathing Apparatus Tender/ Control Unit reg. no. EHW 746K built by Oldland Motor Bodies
(photo – Mike Lawmon)

1973 Dodge K1050 Hydraulic Platform reg. no. FHY 197K built by HCB-A and fitted with Simon SS85 booms (photo – Colin Dunford)

County of Avon Fire Brigade 1974-1996

The County of Avon Fire Brigade was formed on 1st April 1974 from the six stations of Bristol Fire Brigade, the City of Bath Fire Brigade's single station, four stations from Gloucestershire Fire Service and fourteen stations from Somerset Fire Brigade.

One of the first decisions to be made by the new fire brigade was to standardise the pumping fleet on the Dodge chassis to be built by HCB-A. Thirteen Water Tenders were supplied between 1975 and 1976 built on the Dodge K850 chassis. Also in 1976 a Major Rescue Tender was built by Wreckers International on a Dodge K1613 chassis. The same Dodge chassis was used in 1978 when Carmichaels delivered two Turntable Ladders fitted with Metz DL30 ladders. HCB-A had also supplied a Rescue Tender in 1978 on Dodge K1113 chassis. With the Dodge K1113 chassis superseding the K850 HCB-A delivered another eleven Water Tenders in the years 1977 and 1978.

By 1980 the Dodge G13 chassis had appeared on the scene and Cheshire Fire Engineering (CFE) supplied a Rescue Tender. Between 1980 and 1984 HCB-A supplied another twelve Water Tenders on the G13 chassis. Also in 1980 a Dodge G1613 Hydraulic Platform was delivered

This 1967 Ford D600 Foam Tender reg. no. KDF 832E built by HCB-A was one of the appliances taken over from Gloucestershire Fire Brigade in 1974 (photo – Bob Smith)

1976 Dodge K1613 Major Rescue Tender reg. no. KTC 601P built by Wreckers International (photo – Bob Smith)

1978 Dodge K1113 Rescue Tender reg. no. RHW 386S built
by HCB-A (photo – Colin Dunford)

1981 Dodge G1613 Hydraulic Platform reg. no. DHY 531W
built by Carmichaels and fitted with Simon SS263 booms
(photo – Mike Lawmon)

1983 Dodge G1313 Water Tender reg. no. NEU 560Y built by
Merryweather (photo – Bob Smith)

fitted with Simon SS220 booms. In 1985 two Prime Movers were built by Saxons on the Dodge G13C chassis and carried Foam Unit pods. Spectra delivered a Breathing Apparatus Support Unit, a Hose Layer and a Control Unit in 1986 all built on the Dodge S56 chassis. Also in 1986 Carmichaels supplied two Turntable Ladders on the Iveco 256D14 chassis using Metz DLK23-12 ladders and Saxons built a Chemical Incident Unit on a Dodge G13C chassis. In 1986 the Dodge name had been rebranded as Renault and by 1989 another seventeen Water Tenders were supplied all on the Renault G13 Chassis. 1988 saw a Land Rover Rail Rescue Support Unit delivered fitted with a set of rail wheels which could be lowered for use on tracks. In 1989 a Rescue Tender was built on a Mercedes-Benz 917 chassis by Fulton & Wylie and Carmichaels delivered an Aerial Ladder Platform on a Scania 93M chassis using Bronto 22-2Ti booms.

A new Major Rescue Tender was built in 1990 by Wreckers International on a Scania 340 chassis and during the period 1990 to 1995 twenty-seven more Water Tenders were built by Saxon this time on the Renault M230-15D chassis. In 1993 three trailer units were built by Ifor Williams Trailers consisting of two Hose Layers and a Welfare Unit all designed to be pulled by Mitsubishi 4x4 vehicles. Meanwhile a number of 'special's delivered included an Operational Support Unit built by W.H. Bence, a Rescue Tender built by Saxons on a Mercedes-Benz 917

1985 Dodge G13C Prime Mover reg. no. B449 VAE loaded with a Bracey foam pod (photo – Mike Lawmon)

1986 Dodge S56 Control Unit reg. no. C857 DEU built by Spectra (photo – Colin Dunford)

1986 Iveco 256D14 Turntable Ladder reg. no. D951 ETC fitted with
Magirus DLK23-12 ladders (photo – Colin Dunford)

1986 Dodge G13 Chemical Incident Unit reg. no. D952 ETC built by
Saxons (photo – Colin Dunford)

1988 Land Rover Rail Rescue Support Unit reg. no.
E669 JOU fitted out by brigade workshops
(photo – Mike Lawmon)

1989 Dodge G13 Water Tender Ladder reg. no. F65
RTC built by Saxons (photo – Colin Dunford)

1989 Mercedes-Benz 917 Rescue Tender reg. no. F835 OHW built by Fulton & Wylie (photo – Mike Lawmon)

1989 Scania 93M 280 Aerial Ladder Platform reg. no. F62 RTC built by Carmichaels and fitted with Bronto 22-2Ti booms (photo – Mike Lawmon)

1990 Scania 340 Major Rescue Tender reg. no. G522 VWS fitted with Wreckers International lifting equipment and a HIAB crane (photo – Mike Lawmon)

1992 Renault M300 Operational Support Unit reg. no. J644 GHY built by G H Bence and carried a Moffett Mounty Forklift Truck (photo – Colin Dunford)

1992 Renault M230-15D Water Tender Ladder reg. no. K750 LWS built by Saxon (photo – Mike Lawmon)

1995 Mercedes-Benz 1524 Turntable Ladder reg. no. N601 LHT built by Angloco and fitted with Metz DLK30PLC 100ft ladders (photo – Mike Lawmon)

1995 Renault G330-26D Rail Support Unit reg. no. N842 HFB
built by W. H. Bence and fitted with a Bracey Curtainsider body
(photo – Mike Lawmon)

chassis, another Rescue Tender again built by Saxons and fitted with a HIAB crane but now on a Renault chassis and two Turntable Ladders built on the Mercedes-Benz 1524 chassis by Angloco using Metz DLK30 ladders. Also delivered in 1995 was an unusual vehicle built by W.H. Bence on a Renault chassis, namely a Rail Support Unit which carried rail trolleys and was jointly owned with Railtrack.

Avon Fire Brigade 1996-2004

The County of Avon was abolished in 1996 and replaced with four smaller councils; Bath and North East Somerset, Bristol, North Somerset and South Gloucestershire but this had no effect on the fire brigade and a combined fire authority was formed. In 1997 Avon Fire Brigade changed to the MAN chassis and Saxon supplied five Water Tenders by 1999. Also in 1997 a Hydraulic Platform was purchased from Angloco built on a Renault chassis using Simon SS220 booms.

Between 2000 and 2004 fourteen Water Tenders were delivered built by Saxons all on the MAN chassis. During this period Saxons also built a Rescue Tender, an Environmental Protection Unit and two Turntable Ladders with Magirus ladders all on various MAN chassis. A new Command Support Unit was built by Saxon on a Mercedes-Benz Sprinter 814D chassis while

1997 Renault Premium 300 Hydraulic Platform reg. no. R648 BHU built by Angloco and fitted with Simon SS220 booms (photo – Mike Lawmon)

One of a batch of fourteen Water Tenders delivered between 2000 and 2004 was this 2001 MAN 14.284 built by Saxons (photo – Mike Lawmon)

This 2002 MAN M2000 14.264f Rescue Tender reg. no. WM02 EKX was built by Saxons (photo – Mike Lawmon)

2003 Mercedes-Benz Sprinter 814D Command Support Unit reg. no. WM03 AYL built by Saxons (photo – Colin Carter)

2003 Land Rover Defender 130 TD5 Line Rescue Unit reg. no. WU53 ECX built by M & A Bodyworks (photo – Colin Carter)

This Breathing Apparatus Support Unit reg. no. WX53 WFW was also built by M & A Bodyworks on a 2003 Ford Transit 125 T430 chassis (photo – Mike Lawmon)

M&A Bodyworks supplied a Land Rover Line Rescue Unit and a Ford Transit Breathing Apparatus Support Unit.

Avon Fire & Rescue Service 2004 -onwards

In late 2004 Saxons ceased trading and went into receivership and the renamed Fire and Rescue Service had to find a new supplier of fire appliances. John Dennis Coachbuilders (JDC) won the contract and between 2004 and 2007 supplied thirteen Water Tenders all built on the MAN LE14.285 chassis. In 2005 JDC had also built a Heavy Rescue Tender on the heavier MAN LE18.280 chassis and a Water Support Unit based on a Ford Ranger 4x4 chassis. Also in 2005 a Command Support Unit was built by Angloco on a MAN LE12.220 chassis. An unusual appliance was purchased in 2007 with the delivery of a Griffon Hovercraft to be used for rescue work on the mudflats of the Severn Estuary and designated as an All Terrain Rescue Unit. Between 2007 and 2013 JDC delivered a further twenty-one Water Tenders now fitted with PolyBilt bodies on various MAN chassis. In 2008 and 2010 two Combined Aerial Rescue Pumps (CARPs) were delivered by JDC built on the Scania P340 6x2 chassis with PolyBilt bodies and fitted with Vema booms. Another Rescue Tender was built by JDC in 2008 on a MAN chassis again with a PolyBilt body complete with a HIAB crane. Two new Turntable Ladders were delivered in 2012 built by Rosenbauer on the Man chassis and fitted with Metz L27 ladders

2005 MAN LE12.220 Command Support Unit reg. no. WX05 VHZ
built by Angloco (photo – Colin Carter)

2005 Ford Ranger Water Rescue Support Unit reg. no. WX05 YTU
built by JDC which tows a Valiant DR-490 Rigid Inflatable Boat
(photo – Mike Lawmon)

The 2007 All Terrain Rescue Unit consists of a Griffon 380TF
Hovercraft carried on a converted Turntable Ladder chassis reg.
no. Y561 XAE (photo – Colin Carter)

One of two Turntable Ladders purchased in 2012 is this
MAN TG-M 15.290 reg. no. WU12 EXG built by Rosenbauer
and fitted with Metz L27 articulated ladders
(photo – Colin Carter)

2013 MAN TG-L 12.250 Water Tender reg. no. WU63 LVA built by
JDC with a PolyBilt body (photo – Colin Carter)

with a third delivered in 2013. In 2013 two new Animal/Water Rescue Units were built and delivered by Angloco based on the Mercedes-Benz Sprinter chassis.

Currently the Avon Fire and Rescue Fire Service is comprised of twenty-three fire stations, eight of which are wholetime crewed, three wholetime/retained crewed, one day crewed/retained and eleven retained crewed. There are over 600 wholetime firefighters and 200 retained firefighters. The front-line fleet includes thirty-four Pumping Appliances, two Combined Aerial Rescue Pumps, three Turntable Ladders, one Rescue Tender, two Command Support Units, eight Prime Movers, three Foam Pods, one Incident Response Unit, two High Volume Pumping pods, two High Volume Hose Layer pods, five Urban Search and Rescue pods, one Mass Decontamination Disrobe pod, one Detection Investigation and Monitoring Unit, three Rescue Boats and twelve other appliances.

CHAPTER 2
CORNWALL

Although there has been one name change the area covered by the fire service in Cornwall has remained virtually unchanged since 1948

Cornwall Fire Brigade 1948-2009
On the 1st April 1948 there were twenty-nine fire stations, twenty-three of which had been pre-war volunteer units. There were also four local fire units, three of which later became retained stations, the fourth closed as did the fire station at St. Agnes and a new station opened at Polruan to cover the Eastern side of the River Fowey. There were over seventy assorted vehicles transferred from the National Fire Service including sixteen pre-war Pumps and Pump Escapes.

Appliances known to have been taken over by Cornwall Fire Brigade in 1948

Built	Type	Chassis/Body	Body	Reg. No.
1934	Pump Escape	Leyland		CV 9673
1934	Pump	Leyland		ACV 48
1936	Pump	Dennis Ace	Braidwood	CAV 697
1937	Pump	Dennis		DAF 178
1937	Pump Escape	Leyland Cub		DCV 78
1937	Pump Escape	Leyland		DCV 730
1937	Pump	Fordson		DCV 801
1937	Pump	Fordson		GJJ 99
1938	Pump	Dennis		ERL 482
1939	Pump	Leyland FK8	Braidwood	FCV 298
1939	Pump	Leyland FK8	Limousine	FCV 637
1939	Pump Escape	Leyland FK8	Braidwood	FCV 697
1940	Pump	Dennis		FRL 253
1940	Pump	Dennis		FRL 395
1940	Pump Escape	Albion	Kerr Drysdale	FRL 516
1940	Pump	Dennis Light 4	New World	FRL 750
1940	Escape Carrying Unit	Fordson		GGK 126
1940	Escape Carrying Unit	Fordson		GGK 136
1941	Emergency Tender (1)	Austin K2		GGN 673
1941	Hose Layer	Fordson		GGU 802
1941	Hose Layer	Fordson		GGU 826
1941	Salvage Tender (1)	Austin K2		GGX 157
1941	Escape Carrying Unit	Fordson		
1941	Escape Carrying Unit	Fordson		

Built	Type	Chassis/Body	Body	Reg. No.
1941	Hosereel Tender (1)	Fordson		GAF 200
1941	Hosereel Tender (1)	Fordson		GLE 88
1941	ATV	Austin K2		GLE 141
1941	ATV	Austin K2		GLE 283
1941	Hosereel Tender (1)	Austin K2		GLE 441
1941	Hose Carrier (1)	Austin K2		GLE 447
1941	ATV	Austin K2		GLE 448
1941	ATV	Austin K2		GLE 449
1941	Hosereel Tender (1)	Austin K2		GLE 592
1941	Hosereel Tender (1)	Austin K2		GLE 643
1942	Escape Carrying Unit	Fordson		
1942	Hosereel Tender (1)	Austin K2		GLR 369
1942	ATV	Austin K2		GLR 485
1942	ATV	Austin K2		GLR 486
1942	ATV	Austin K2		GLR 782
1942	ATV	Austin K2		GLR 938
1942	ATV	Austin K2		GLR 939
1942	Salvage Tender (1)	Austin K2		GLT 101
1942	ATV	Austin K2		GLT 613
1942	ATV	Austin K2		GLT 629
1942	Canteen Van (1)	Austin K2		GLR 631
1943	Escape Carrying Unit	Austin K4		GXA 706
1943	Escape Carrying Unit	Austin K4		GXA 724
1943	Escape Carrying Unit	Austin K4		GLA 745
1943	ATV	Austin K2		GXH 83
1943	ATV	Austin K2		GXH 143
1943	ATV	Austin K2		GXH 83
1943	ATV	Austin K2		GXH 143
1943	ATV	Austin K2		GXH 145
1943	ATV	Austin K2		GXH 147
1943	Hosereel Tender (1)	Austin K2		GXH 300
1943	ATV	Austin K2		GXH 613
1943	ATV	Austin K2		GXH 147
1943	Hosereel Tender (1)	Austin K2		GXH 667
1943	Hosereel Tender (1)	Austin K2		GXH 668
1943	Hosereel Tender (1)	Austin K2		GXH 996
1943	Hosereel Tender (1)	Austin K2		GXH 668
1943	Water Carrier (2)	Austin K4		GXM 104
1943	Water Carrier (2)	Austin K4		GXM 105
1943	Water Carrier (2)	Austin K4		GXM 106
1943	Water Carrier (2)	Austin K4		GXM 109
1943	Escape Carrying Unit	Austin K4		GXM 157
1943	Water Tender A (2)	Fordson		GXM 202
1943	Water Tender A (2)	Fordson		GXM 326
1943	Turntable Ladder	Austin K4	Merryweather 60ft	GXN 203
1943	Water Tender A (2)	Dodge		GXO 545
1943	Water Tender A (2)	Dodge		GXO 561

Built	Type	Chassis/Body	Body	Reg. No.
1943	Water Tender A (2)	Dodge		GXO 563
1943	Water Tender A (2)	Dodge		GXO 567
1943	Water Tender A (2)	Dodge		GYR 491
1946	Bedford	Breakdown Lorry		GYR 99

(1)   Converted from ATV
(2)   Converted from Major Dam Unit

This 1939 Leyland FK8 Pump reg. no. FCV 637 was one of the pre-war appliances taken over by Cornwall in 1948 and served until 1960.
(Unknown photographer)

1941 Austin K2 Hosereel Tender reg. no. GLE 441 converted from an ATV and trailer pump (Unknown photographer)

Between 1949 and 1953 twenty-nine 'A' type Water Tenders were purchased built on the Austin K4 Loadstar chassis with Home Office bodywork and eight Pump Escapes on the same chassis but built by Hampshire Car Bodies (HCB). In 1953 the brigades Water Tenders were converted to 'B' type Water Tenders by the Home Office workshops in Swindon. Three Dennis F8 Water Tenders were bought in 1955 and then in 1957 the first Light Pump was introduced based on an Austin Champ chassis and built by Fire Armour. Following the success of the Austin Champ a total of thirty Light Pumps were purchased between 1958 and 1965 but now built on the Austin Gipsy chassis. A Control Unit was also supplied in 1959 again based on an Austin Gipsy.

A local company, Drakes, supplied a number of appliances to Cornwall in the early 1960s including a Water Tender Escape built on an Austin A503 chassis, two Water Carriers, two Pump/Hose Carriers and a Pump Ladder all built on the Austin FFG chassis. In 1966 Cornwall Fire Brigade purchased two appliances from Exeter City Fire Brigade; a 1953 Dennis F8 Water

1950 Austin Loadstar Water Tender reg. no. NCV 417 built at the Home Office workshops, Swindon (The Roy Yeoman Collection)

1959 Austin Gipsy L4P reg. no. 82 ERL based at Saltash Fire Station (The Roy Yeoman Collection)

1960 Austin A503 Water Tender Escape reg. no. 586 HCV built by Drakes (The Roy Yeoman Collection)

1961 Austin FFG Foam Tender reg. no. 233 NAF originally built by Drakes as a Pump/Hose Carrier (The Roy Yeoman Collection)

In 1966 Cornwall bought this 1953 Dennis F8 Water Tender reg. no. OFJ 333 from Exeter City Fire Brigade
(photo – Mike Lawmon)

One of a trio on the run In Cornwall was this 1968 Bedford TJ4LZ Emergency Tender reg. no. NRL 385F built by HCB-Angus (photo – Gary Chapman)

This 1960 Bedford RLHZ ex-AFS Recovery Vehicle reg. no. 373 ALC was obtained by Cornwall Fire Brigade in 1968 (photo - Gary Chapman)

1969 Bedford TJ4LZ Water Tender reg. no. PCV 478G built by HCB-Angus (The Roy Yeoman Collection)

1971 Leyland Laird Water Carrier reg. no. YAF 725J built by Fergusons (The Roy Yeoman Collection)

Tender and a 1956 Bedford TJ4LZ Water Tender. The same year a contract had been signed with HCB-Angus (HCB-A) and by 1971 nineteen Water Tenders and three Emergency Tenders had been delivered all built on the Bedford TJ4LZ chassis. An ex-AFS Recovery Vehicle was obtained in 1968 and operated by brigade workshops.

A Cliff Rescue Tender had been built in 1970 by Cornwall's workshops using a BMC J4 vehicle and an ex-demonstrator Land Rover L4P with Bainbridge bodywork was purchased in 1971. A Leyland Laird Water Carrier was delivered in 1971 with two more based on the Leyland Boxer chassis being delivered in 1972 and 1973. Between 1972 and 1973 saw a new name in the fleet when eight Dennis DJ Water Tenders were purchased. Also in 1973 HCB-A supplied a Land Rover L4P. Another ex-demonstrator was obtained in 1974 this time from HCB-A built on a Bedford TKEL chassis. The first new aerial appliance supplied to Cornwall came in 1974 in the shape of a Hydraulic Platform built on a Dodge K1050 chassis by HCB-A with Simon SS220 booms. Also in 1974 Carmichaels supplied a L6P built on a Range Rover 6x4 chassis. HCB-A continued to be the supplier of pumping appliances and between 1974 and 1975 delivered seven Water Tenders all built on the Dodge K850 chassis. HCB-A also supplied three Land Rover appliances in 1976. 1977 saw a major change when Eagle Engineering built four Water Tenders on the Bedford TK chassis followed by four more in 1978. Two Water Tenders were delivered in 1979 by HCB-A on the Bedford TK chassis one with a Crew Safety Cab.

1972 Dennis DJ Water Tender Ladder reg. no. BAF 55K. (The Roy Yeoman Collection)

1973 Land Rover 108 L4P reg. no. JCV 86L built by HCB-Angus. (The Roy Yeoman Collection)

1974 Dodge K1050 Hydraulic Platform reg. no. RCV 273M built by HCB-Angus and fitted with Simon SS220 booms (photo – Mike Lawmon)

Polruan's 1974 Range Rover L6P built by Carmichaels reg. no. HAF 481N. (photo – Gary Chapman)

1980 saw the delivery of two Bedford TK Water Tenders built by HCB-A and the delivery of a Dennis RS133 Water Tender which was to become the last Dennis appliance in Cornwall's fleet. Between 1979 and 1980 twelve L4Ps were built by Carmichaels on the Land Rover Series III chassis. Cheshire Fire Engineering (CFE) supplied two Water Tenders and an Emergency Tender in 1982 built on the Bedford TK chassis. Between 1983 and 1984 HCB-A delivered four Water Tenders and two Emergency Tenders built on the Bedford TK chassis which were the last of the Bedford appliances with the Renault-Dodge G13 becoming the preferred chassis.

By 1990 a total of sixteen Water Tenders had been supplied by HCB-A with three supplied by Saxon. Meanwhile between 1983 and 1990 Cornwall's own workshops had built a total of eighteen Land Rover based appliances and three Water Carriers on the Renault-Dodge G16 chassis. In 1990 there was again a change in the chassis supplier this time to Mercedes-Benz when HCB-A built four Water Tenders on the 1222F chassis. Also the same year Saxons built a Hydraulic Platform on a Mercedes-Benz 1625 chassis using the Simon SS220 booms from the 1974 Dodge K1050 appliance. The Dodge chassis was then converted by brigade workshops into a Recovery Vehicle and fitted with a Hiab crane. 1991 saw Cornwall's workshops fitting out a Peugeot Express van as a Breathing Apparatus Support Unit and the purchase of a Midi Water Tender built on a Dodge S75 chassis. In 1992 a Kawasaki Mule All Terrain Vehicle was converted by workshops which was towed on a trailer and designed for use in the narrow streets of Looe and the seaside village of Polperro. Cornwall's workshops also built an Incident Control Unit in 1993 based on a Mercedes-Benz 814D chassis. The use of the Mercedes-Benz 1120AF and the 1124F chassis continued throughout the 1990s with Carmichaels supplying eighteen Water Tenders, HCB-A supplying four before going out of business in 1994 and Saxon

Another ex-demonstrator appliance was this 1979 Bedford TKEL Water Tender Ladder reg. no. MAA 654T built by HCB-A with a Crew Safety Cab .(photo – Mike Lawmon)

1980 Dennis RS133 Water Tender Ladder reg. no. CGL 37V. (photo – Gary Chapman)

1982 Bedford TKG Emergency Tender reg. no. NGL 848X built by Cheshire Fire Engineering. (The Roy Yeoman Collection)

1983 Bedford TK1260 Water Tender Ladder reg. no. PRL 374Y built by HCB-A. (photo – Gary Chapman)

This 1984 Bedford TKEL Emergency Tender reg. no. A987 KCV was built by HCB-A. (photo – Colin Dunford)

1989 Renault-Dodge G17 Water Carrier reg. no. F326 XAF built by Fergusson. photo – Colin Dunford)

1990 Renault Dodge G13T Water Tender Ladder reg. no. G745 CAF built by HCB-A. (photo – Gary Chapman)

The former Dodge K1050 Hydraulic Platform after removal of the booms and conversion to a Recovery Vehicle. (photo – Gary Chapman)

This 1991 Dodge S75 Midi Water Tender reg. no. H625 FGL was purchased specifically for Polruan Fire Station. (photo – Gary Chapman)

Specially ordered for the narrow streets of Looe and Polperro was this 1992 Kawasaki Mule All Terrain Vehicle reg. no. J752 KAF. (photo – Colin Dunford)

For many years Cornwall's Control Unit was this 1993 Mercedes-Benz 814D fitted out by Brigade workshops. (photo – Mike Lawmon)

1994 Mercedes-Benz 1120AF 4- wheel drive Water Tender Ladder reg. no. L214 VRL with HCB-A bodywork. (photo – Gary Chapman)

supplying six. In 1995 Cornwall's first Aerial Ladder Platform was built by Bedwas on a Mercedes-Benz 2532 chassis fitted with Simon ST290-S booms. Cornwall's workshops fitted out a Vauxhall Brava as a L4P in 1995 and then in 1996 converted two Mercedes-Benz 412D vans into a Breathing Apparatus Unit and an Operational Support Vehicle. Carmichaels delivered two Rescue Tenders in 1997 both built on the Mercedes-Benz 1124AF chassis. Another Aerial Ladder Platform was purchased in 1997 again built by Bedwas but this time built on a Mercedes-

Benz 1827 chassis with Simon SS240 booms. In 1999 another Breathing Apparatus Unit was built by Cornwall's workshops by converting a Mercedes-Benz Vito van. In 1999 a Co-Responder Scheme was introduced in conjunction with the South West Ambulance Service to provide basic life support until an ambulance arrives on scene.

The new millennium saw the arrival of the first Mercedes-Benz Atego 1328 Water Tender and by 2011 a total of twenty were delivered, seven built by Carmichaels and thirteen built by John Dennis Coachbuilders (JDC). Two Operational Support Vehicles were purchased in 2002 and 2003 built on the Mercedes-Benz Sprinter chassis which combined the roles of Environmental Protection, BA Support and Water Rescue. Carmichaels continued to build L4Ps delivering seven Vauxhall Bravas and four Toyota Hiluxs. In 2004 three Water Carriers were built on the Mercedes-Benz Atego 1828 chassis with Crossland Tankers bodywork. Also in 2004 a change was made to the supplier of L4Ps, now designated as Light Pumping Appliances (LPAs) when

1997 Mercedes-Benz 1124AF Rescue Tender reg. no. P136 PCV built by Carmichaels and fitted with a Palfinger crane.
(photo – Colin Dunford)

1997 Mercedes-Benz 1827 Aerial Ladder Platform reg. no. P138 PCV built by Bedwas and fitted with Simon SS24 booms.
(photo – Gary Chapman)

This former 1999 Vauxhall Brava 4x4 L4P reg. no. T590 KCV
is seen here in use for Co-Responding duties.
(photo – Colin Dunford)

2000 Mercedes-Benz Atego 1328 Water Tender Ladder built
by JDC reg. no. X198 UCV. (photo – Gary Chapman)

2001 Mercedes-Benz Sprinter 312D 4x4 Operational Support
Vehicle reg. no. WK51 CWU. (photo – Gary Chapman)

One of three Water Carriers delivered in 2004 is Mercedes-Benz
Atego 1828 reg. no. WK53 BRV built by Crosland Tankers.
(photo – Gary Chapman)

2005 Toyota Hilux 280 Light Pumping Appliance built by
Excalibur reg. no. WK54 ETY. (photo – Gary Chapman)

2007 Mercedes-Benz Unimog U500 Water Tender Ladder built
by JDC with a Plastisol body reg. no. WK57 AAN.
(photo – Gary Chapman)

Excalibur built five on the Toyota Hilux chassis. Two Environmental Support Vehicles were built by Cornwall's workshops in 2005 by converting Vauxhall Movano vans.

Following the serious flooding in the Boscastle area in 2004 the brigade carried out an investigation into its capabilities of dealing with similar incidents. The result was an order for a Mercedes-Benz Unimog Water Tender, capable of driving through deep water, which was built by JDC and delivered in 2007 to Launceston Fire Station.

Cornwall Fire & Rescue Service 2009 - onwards

Cornwall Fire Brigade was renamed a Fire and Rescue Service in 2009 in line with new government guidelines.

In 2010 two Command Support Vehicles built on the Mercedes-Benz Sprinter van chassis were delivered followed the same year by a Welfare Unit built on a Mitsubishi Fuso Canter chassis which combines both kitchen and toilet facilities. Also in 2010 one Line Rescue Tender and two Rescue Tenders were built by JDC all on the Mercedes-Benz Atego 1329f chassis with Polybilt bodywork. Two new Aerial Ladder Platforms were built by JDC on the MAN 26.360 chassis

Cornwall has two Command Support Vehicles. This one which is based at Launceston is a 2010 Mercedes-Benz Sprinter reg. no. WK59 DZN built by Bott. (photo – Gary Chapman)

Cornwall's Welfare Unit is this 2010 Mitsubishi Fuso Canter reg. no. WK59 AKP. (photo – Gary Chapman)

One of a pair of Aerial Ladder Platforms is this 2010 MAN
TGS26.360 reg. no. WK59 BPZ built by JDC and fitted with Vema
343TFL booms. (photo – Gary Chapman)

This Vauxhall Corsa Combo reg. no. WK11 ATZ is one of the
vehicles used for Co-Responding with the South West Ambulance
Service. (photo – Michael Sones)

One of three Volvo FLL290 Water Tender Ladders built by JDC and
delivered in 2014. (photo – Michael Sones)

using Vema booms and delivered in 2010 and 2012. Meanwhile in 2011 a new Kawasaki Mule All Terrain Vehicle was purchased to replace the earlier version delivered in 1991. Eight Water Rescue Units based on the Toyota HiLux chassis were purchased between 2011 and 2013. These were fitted out by workshops and operate in pairs with one of each pair carrying an inflatable boat. A new era dawned in 2014 with an order for six Volvo FLL290 Water Tender Ladders built by JDC. Three were delivered in 2014 with a further three in 2015.

Currently Cornwall Fire and Rescue Service operates from thirty-one fire stations two of which are wholetime/retained, five day-crewed/retained and the remaining twenty-four retained crewed. Front-line appliances include thirty-one Water Tender Ladders, twelve Water Tenders, twenty-two Light Pumping Appliances, three Water Carriers, two Aerial Ladder Platforms, two Rescue Tenders, two Line Rescue Tenders, eight Water Rescue Units, two Operational Support Vehicles, two Environmental Support Vehicles, two Command Support Vehicles, an All Terrain Vehicle, two Incident Response Units, three Prime Movers, one High Volume Pumping Unit pod, one High Volume Hose Layer Unit pod and a Mass Decontamination Disrobe pod.

CHAPTER 3
DEVON AND SOMERSET

The two counties covered in this chapter have gone through many changes in fire cover from the time of de-nationalisation in 1948 through to the current time.

The 1947 Fire Services Act set out the criteria for the formation of fire brigades. As independent cities both Exeter and Plymouth formed their own brigades separate from the remainder of the county of Devon. Following local government re-organisation in 1973 all three authorities were amalgamated into one of the largest 'shire' brigades in the UK with fifty-eight fire stations and over eighty fire appliances.

When Somerset Fire Brigade was formed in 1948 it consisted of forty-one fire stations but by 1970 the number had dropped to thirty-eight with the closure of a retained station at Watchet and volunteer stations at Milborne Port and Wedmore. When the new Avon Fire Brigade was created in 1974 all but one station in Somerset's "A" Division was transferred to Avon.

The final amalgamation occurred in 2007 when both counties formed a combined fire authority renamed Devon and Somerset Fire & Rescue Service.

Devon County Fire Service 1948-1973
Pre-NFS appliances known to have been taken over by Devon County Fire Service

Built	Type	Chassis	Body	Reg. No.
1930	Pump Escape	Albion	Merryweather	DV 6228
1934	Pump	Leyland Cub FK4		BTA 850
1935	Pump	Dennis Ace		BUO 514
1936	Pump Escape	Albion	Merryweather	AOD 637
1937	Pump Escape	Dennis Light 6		CTT 45
1937	Pump	Dennis Light 6		FFJ 187
1938	Pump Escape	Leyland Cub FK6		DTT 311
1938	Pump Escape	Morris Commercial	Merryweather	EUO 881
1938	Pump Escape	Leyland Cub FK6		CDV 592
1938	Pump	Merryweather		CDV 799
1939	Pump	Leyland Cub FK8		DOD 37
1939	Turntable Ladder	Leyland TLM	Metz 100 feet	EDV 499
1940	Pump Escape	Leyland Cub FK8		EOD 267
1940	Pump	Leyland Cub FK8		EOD 168
1940	Pump	Albion	Kerr Drysdale	FTA 51
1940	Pump	Leyland Cub FK8		FTA 73
1940	Pump	Leyland Cub FK8		EOD 158

Following the transfer from the National Fire Service (NFS) to the new Devon County Fire Service on the 1st April 1948 there were a number of station closures and at the same time some new stations opened during a period of consolidation. The new service consisted of five wholetime/retained stations, 48 retained stations and three volunteer stations. Many of the buildings were antiquated, too small to house modern appliances or to provide the necessary accommodation. With no new fire appliances being built it became necessary to adapt ex-wartime vehicles. Two such conversions formed the backbone of the new service.

Former Austin K2 Auxiliary Towing Vehicles (ATVs) were taken over by Devon and used in conjunction with Trailer Pumps as Hosereel Tenders. A 150 gallon water tank was installed within the body and a small pump fitted to supply a hosereel. Ladders were carried on the roof with other equipment carried within the van type body. Another two ATVs were converted into Salvage Tenders and a third converted to an Emergency Salvage Tender.

Mobile Dam Units and Heavy Units based on Austin K4, Bedford QL, Dodge and Fordson 7v chassis were converted to Water Tenders by mounting a 400 gallon water tank on the chassis with a self-contained fire pump fitted with connections to the tank and a hosereel. An extension

1938 Leyland Cub FK6 Pump reg. no. CDV 592 seen here in preservation (The Roy Yeoman Collection)

1940 Leyland TLM Turntable Ladder reg. no. EDV 499 - note the five section Metz ladders fitted to ease turn-outs from the old Torquay Fire Station (The Roy Yeoman Collection)

ladder and a short ladder were carried and stowage for hose and other equipment was fitted within new bodywork. A separate trailer pump was towed by these 'A' type Water Tenders.

Eight Escape Carrying Units based on the Austin K4 and Fordson 7V chassis were converted to Pump Escapes by adding Barton front-mounted pumps. The final appliance taken over was an Austin K4 Turntable Ladder fitted with a hand operated Merryweather 60 feet ladders.

The first new post-war appliances were two Commer Water Tenders built by Whitsons in 1950 followed by two built by Carmichaels in 1950 and 1951. With the introduction of the Dennis F series appliances a Pump Escape was purchased from Dennis Bros on the F12 chassis. By now Water Tenders had built in fire pumps and there was no need for a separate trailer pump and they were now classified as 'B' type Water Tenders. Between 1952 and 1955 Devon was to purchase eighteen of the Dennis F8 Water Tenders. The next batch of four Water Tenders was built in 1956 by Hampshire Car Bodies (HCB) on the Dodge Kew chassis. 1957 saw Devon revert back to the Dennis chassis when four F25 Water Tenders were purchased. HCB then supplied a batch of fifteen Water Tenders between 1957and 1961 built on the Dodge chassis.

1950 Commer QX Water Tender reg. no. MTA 40 built by Whitsons, seen here when in the reserve fleet (The Roy Yeoman Collection)

Hose Layer reg. no. STT 319 converted from a 1955 F8 Water Tender (The Roy Yeoman Collection)

One of four delivered in 1956 was this Dodge Kew Water Tender reg. no. UUO 304 built by HCB with an unpainted all alloy finish (The Roy Yeoman Collection)

1957 Dennis F25 Water Tender reg. no. VOD 574 (The Roy Yeoman Collection)

This Dodge forward control Water Tender reg. no. 11 COD was built by HCB in 1960 again with an unpainted alloy finish (The Roy Yeoman Collection)

Bedford based appliances were introduced into the Devon fleet in 1961 when HCB built two Water Tenders on the Bedford J4 chassis and by 1965 a total of eighteen had been supplied. HCB built two Water Tender Escapes in 1961 and 1963 this time on the Bedford J5 chassis. For the smaller retained stations Pump Hosereel Tenders were built by HCB which had quite basic bodywork and were nicknamed affectionately as 'breadvans'. Six of these were built between 1961 and 1967 on the Bedford J2 chassis. 1965 saw the introduction of a unique firefighting appliance when the 60 feet ladders from the wartime Austin K4 Turntable Ladder were modified for power operation and mounted on the rear of a Bedford TK chassis. It was equipped with HCB bodywork incorporating a six man crew cab, a pump and equipment lockers. It remained in service at Ilfracombe until replaced in the early 1980s. A conventional Turntable Ladder was also purchased in 1965 built on an AEC Mercury chassis with 100 feet Merryweather ladders. By 1966 HCB had become HCB-Angus (HCB-A) and supplied an Emergency Salvage Tender based on the Bedford TK chassis followed by a similar vehicle in 1967. Six more Water Tenders were built on the Bedford J5 chassis by HCB-A in 1967. The same manufacturer delivered a Pump Escape in 1969 to replace the Dennis F12 purchased back in 1951 and nineteen Water Tenders between 1969 and 1973 all built on the Bedford TKEL chassis.

Nicknamed 'breadvans' this 1961 Bedford J2 Pump Hosereel Tender reg. no. 997 NUO was one of six built by HCB
(The Roy Yeoman Collection)

The 1965 Bedford TK Pump/Turntable Ladder reg. no. CTA 298C built by HCB using the 60 feet Merryweather ladders from a wartime appliance (The Roy Yeoman Collection)

1965 AEC Mercury Turntable Ladder reg. no. CTA 297C fitted with
Merryweather 100 feet ladders. (The Roy Yeoman Collection)

City of Exeter Fire Brigade 1948-1973

Appliances known to have to have been taken over by City of Exeter Fire Brigade in 1948

Built	Type	Chassis	Body	Reg. No.
1934	Pump Escape	Albion	Merryweather	AFJ 281
1938	Pump	Leyland Cub FK6		EFJ 359
1943	Pump Escape	Austin K4		GXM 156
1943	Water Tender (1)	Dodge		GXM 574
1943	Emergency Tender	Austin K2		GXH 572
1943	ATV (2)	Austin K2		GXH 805
1943	ATV	Austin K2		GLT 492
1943	Hose Carrier	Austin K2		GXH 674
1943	Turntable Ladder	Leyland Beaver	Merryweather 100 ft	GXA 69

(1)   Later converted to a Water Carrier
(2)   Later converted to an Emergency Tender

When formed on 1st April 1948 Exeter became one of the smallest brigades in the country with just one fire station at Danes Castle which was wholetime manned backed up by a retained complement. The fleet included four pumping appliances, a Turntable Ladder and an Emergency Tender which were a mixture of pre-war and wartime appliances.

The first appliance supplied to Exeter Fire Brigade was not in fact new but a 1937 Leyland Cub Pump Escape which came from Cornwall County Fire Brigade in exchange for a large trailer Pump!   The first new appliance was a 1953 Dennis F8 Water Tender followed in 1956 with the commencement of the supply of Bedford Dual Purpose Appliances which could be used as either Pump Escapes or Pumps. Two were build in 1956 and 1959 on the Bedford SH chassis by Miles Brothers of Cheltenham and between 1962 and 1967 four more were supplied built on the Bedford TK chassis by HCB later HCB-A.

In 1960 a new Water Carrier had been built on a Bedford R chassis by the brigade's workshops utilising the tank from the wartime vehicle. 1964 saw the replacement of the wartime Turntable Ladder with 100 feet Merryweather ladders built on an AEC Mercury chassis. Also in 1964 the brigade purchased a new Emergency Tender built on a Bedford TK chassis by Mumfords of Plymouth. Workshops carried out another conversion in 1969 converting an ex-Civil Defence Ford Thames vehicle into a Control/Salvage Unit.

1961 Bedford TK Dual Purpose Appliance reg. no. 444 EFJ
built by HCB and seen here in Exeter City Centre
(The Roy Yeoman Collection)

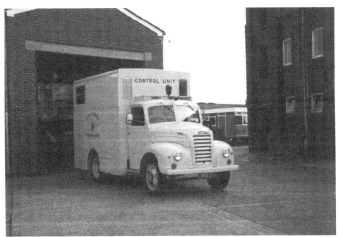

In 1969 Exeter City Fire Brigade purchased this 1955 ex-Civil
Defence Ford Thames reg. no. RYX 173 for use as a Control
Unit (The Roy Yeoman Collection)

1972 Dennis F49 Water Tender built by Dennis Bros.
(The Roy Yeoman Collection)

With the building of multi-storey car parks the brigade purchased a Light 4x4 Pump built by Carmichaels on a Land Rover short wheelbase chassis in 1971 to deal with fires in these and other similar inaccessible areas. The final appliance purchased by the city brigade was a 1972 Dennis F49 Water Tender.

City of Plymouth Fire Brigade 1948-1973

The Plymouth City Fire Brigade had four fire stations with a complement of around 250 wholetime men. The headquarters was at Station 'A' Greenbank and the appliance fleet consisted of a mixture of pre-war and ex-NFS vehicles.

Station A Greenbank

Built	Type	Chassis	Body	Reg. No.
1932	Pump Escape	Dennis Big 6		JY 956
1938	Emergency Tender	Bedford		ADR 561
1941	Turntable Ladder	Leyland	Merryweather 100ft	CDR 287
1943	Salvage Tender	Austin K2		GLT 615
1943	Foam Tender	Austin K4		GHX 681
1943	Radio Van	Ford 7v		

Station B Penlee

Built	Type	Chassis	Body	Reg. No.
1930	Pump	Dennis		DR 7555
1942	Turntable Ladder	Leyland TD7	Merryweather 100ft	FDR 706
1942	Hose Carrier	Austin K2		GLT 610
1943	Pump Escape	Austin K4		GXA 740
1943	Radio Van	Fordson 7v		
1944	Amphibious Unit (1)	GMC DUKW		XHO 272

(1)   Carried portable pumps

Station C Torr

Built	Type	Chassis	Body	Reg. No.
1938	Pump Escape	Leyland Cub FK6		AJY 747
1941	Escape Carrying Unit	Fordson 7v		GGN 749
1941	Hose Carrier/Lighting	Fordson 7v		GGU 815
1943	Water Tender	Austin K4		GXM 93
1943	Radio Van	Ford 7v		
1943	Canteen Van	Austin K3		

Station D Boathouse

Built	Type	Chassis	Body	Reg. No.
1939	Pump	Fordson 7v		GLT 235
1941	ATV & Trailer Pump	Austin K4		GGX 429
1941	ATV & Trailer Pump	Austin K4		GXH 144
1943	Fireboat 'Iris' (2)	Taylor		

(2)   Later renamed Cissie Brock

This 1938 Bedford Emergency Tender reg. no. ADR 561 was converted from a horse box (The Roy Yeoman Collection)

Penlee's 1942 Leyland Titan TD7 Turntable Ladder reg. no. FDR 706 (The Roy Yeoman Collection)

Plymouth's Fireboat *The Cissie Brock* built in 1943 by Taylors of Chertsey (The Roy Yeoman Collection)

1955 Dennis F8 Water Tender reg. no. LCO 318 now in preservation (photo - Mike Williams)

Modernisation of the fleet and replacement of old fire stations was quicker in Plymouth than elsewhere in Devon and most of the pre-war open bodied machines had been replaced with enclosed appliances by the mid 1950s. The first new appliance purchased by Plymouth was a Dennis F12 Pump Escape in 1951 followed by two identical appliances in 1953. Between 1955 and 1958 three Dennis F8 Water Tenders were the next additions to the fleet. The 1941 Leyland Turntable Ladder was replaced in 1961 by an AEC Mercury appliance fitted with 100 feet Merryweather ladders. In 1963 a local coachbuilder, Mumfords, supplied two appliances built on the Bedford TK chassis; a Water Tender and an Emergency/Salvage Tender. These were followed in 1965 by a Hose/Foam Tender built by HCB. The 1942 half-cab Leyland Turntable Ladder was replaced by a Simon Hydraulic Platform, built by Carmichaels on a Leyland Beaver chassis, at the new Camel's Head Fire Station in 1967.

In April 1967 the Plymouth City area was enlarged to include Plympton and Plymstock and their two retained stations passed from Devon County to Plymouth City. Plympton had a 1964 Bedford J5 Water Tender built by HCB whilst Plymstock had a 1953 Dennis F8 Water Tender.

In 1968 a new innovative concept was introduced, the 'Multi-Purpose Appliance', to carry out most of the functions of a pump escape, a water tender, an emergency tender and a salvage tender.

1963 Bedford TK Emergency Salvage Tender reg. no. VJY 999 built by Mumfords and seen here in the Devon Fire Brigade livery (The Roy Yeoman Collection)

1967 Leyland Beaver Hydraulic Platform reg. no. HCO 999F built by Carmichaels and fitted with Simon SS65 booms (The Roy Yeoman Collection)

1969 Leyland Beaver Multi-Purpose Pump reg. no. KJY 999G
built by Carmichaels photographed after the amalgamation into
Devon Fire Brigade (The Roy Yeoman Collection)

It carried an alloy 13.5 metre rescue ladder, a Bayley wooden extension ladder, roof and short extension ladders, together with hydraulic rescue equipment, power cutting equipment and electrical lighting. Between 1968 and 1972 seven of these appliances were purchased all built by Carmichaels on the Leyland Beaver chassis. In 1970 a Special Equipment Tender was built by Hawsons on a Bedford van chassis, an Emergency Tender in all but name, and known by the crews as the bread van. Another two 'Multi-Purpose Appliances' were ordered in 1973 built on the Dennis F108 chassis but not delivered until after amalgamation into the new Devon Fire Brigade.

Devon Fire Brigade 1973-1987

The new Devon Fire Brigade was formed by the amalgamation of the Devon County Fire Brigade, the City of Exeter Fire Brigade and the City of Plymouth Fire Brigade.

The first appliances delivered were the two 'Multi-Purpose Appliances' which had already been ordered by Plymouth Fire Brigade. One of the early decisions to be made was with regard to road traffic accidents. The old policy was to attend with one pumping appliance and the nearest Emergency Tender (ET) which with only four ETs in the county put a heavy workload on these resources. It was decided that every station in the brigade should have at least one 'Multi-Purpose Appliance' based on the Plymouth design but it was soon realised that the Plymouth appliances built on the 16 ton Leyland Beaver chassis and about eight feet wide would be too unwieldy in the rural Devon lanes. Forty-six new Devon 'Multi-Purpose Appliances' were delivered between 1974 and 1979 built on the Dennis D chassis. During 1976 a batch of nine were built by HCB-A on the Commer Commando chassis with the final batch of six built on the Dodge G13 chassis again by HCB-A. A Land Rover L4P was built in 1979 by Carmichaels for the volunteer station at Kingston.

1980 saw two Emergency Tender/Control Units purchased, both built on the Dodge G13 chassis by Bensons. In 1981 two new Turntable Ladders built on the Shelvoke & Drewry WX chassis were delivered built by G & T Fire Control and fitted with the Merryweather ladders from the earlier AEC Mercury appliances. A similar appliance was delivered in 1982. Also in 1982 the booms from the 1967 Leyland Beaver Hydraulic Platform were re-chassied onto another Shelvoke & Drewry WX chassis by Carmichaels. Two more Turntable Ladders were supplied; the first in 1983 built by Angloco on a Shelvoke & Drewry WX chassis with 100 feet Metz ladders and the second in 1985 built by Carmichael with 100 feet Magirus ladders. By 1982 the term 'Multi-Purpose Appliance' had been dropped and reverted to Water Tender and six were delivered built

1976 Commer Commando Multi-Purpose Pump reg. no. LTT 203P (The Roy Yeoman Collection)

1978 Dennis D Multi-Purpose Pump reg. no. XTT 307S (photo – Colin Dunford)

1979 Land Rover Series III L4P reg. no. YCV 942T built by Carmichaels and ordered for the Kingston volunteer fire station (photo – Gary Chapman)

on the Dodge G1213 chassis by Carmichaels. By 1983 the older Dodge and Dennis appliances were being replaced by Dennis RS133 appliances and thirteen were supplied over the next two years. Two more Emergency Tender/Control Units were delivered in 1984 this time built by Angloco on the Dodge G12 chassis. In 1985 thirteen Water Tenders were delivered on the newer Dennis RS135 chassis. Up until now all Dennis based appliances had all been built in the Dennis factory at Guildford but in 1985 the company stopped building appliance bodies and only supplied the chassis. Three Hose Layers had been purchased for Devon Fire Brigade; the first in 1981 built by G & T Fire Control on a Ford A0609 4x4 chassis, the second was delivered by Fulton & Wylie on a similar chassis in 1983 whilst the third was built in 1985 by Angloco on a Dodge S75C 4x4 chassis. Also in 1985 Carmichaels delivered an Iveco 265 Turntable Ladder fitted with Magirus ladders. A combined Hose Layer/Foam Tender was built and delivered by Saxon-Sandbech in 1986 on a Dodge G13 4x4 chassis. The final appliances delivered to Devon Fire Brigade were seven Water Tenders built by Saxon-Sandbech on the Dennis RS135 chassis in 1986.

1982 Shelvoke & Drewry WY Turntable Ladder reg. no. VDV 143X built by G&T with Merryweather ladders (photo – Colin Dunford)

1984 Dennis RS133 Water Tender Ladder reg. no. A665 KFJ built by Dennis Bros (photo – Colin Dunford)

1984 Dodge G12 Emergency Tender reg. no. A975 NDV built by Angloco (The Roy Yeoman Collection)

1985 Dodge S75C Hose Layer reg. no. B317 VFJ built by Angloco (The Roy Yeoman Collection)

Carmichaels delivered this Iveco 265 Turntable Ladder reg. no.
B318 VFJ and fitted with Magirus ladders in 1985
(photo – Colin Dunford)

1989 Dennis F127 Turntable Ladder reg. no. F650 JFJ built by JDC
and fitted with Camiva ladders (photo – Colin Dunford)

Devon Fire & Rescue Service 1987-2007

In order to reflect the wider role of the modern fire service the brigade was renamed Devon Fire and Rescue Service in 1987.

In 1988 two more batches of Dennis RS135 appliances were delivered, seven built by Angloco and seven by John Dennis Coachbuilders (JDC). 1989 saw the delivery of a Turntable Ladder built by JDC on the Dennis F127 chassis and fitted with French Camiva ladders. A change to the pumping fleet occurred in 1989 when seven Volvo FL6.14 appliances were built by Saxon-Sandbech.

In 1991 another batch of nine Dennis RS Water Tenders were built by JDC. Three Aerial Ladder Platforms were supplied by Angloco between 1990 and 1992 built on the Volvo FL10 6x4 chassis and fitted with Bronto 28-2Ti booms. During this period it became necessary to find a new smaller appliance for those stations that could not house an RS based appliance and the answer was the Dennis DS155 which was only seven feet wide and twelve were built by JDC between 1991 and 1992. 1994 saw the delivery of a new Turntable Ladder built by GB Fire on an

One of seven delivered in 1989 was this Volvo FL6.14 Water
Tender Ladder reg. no. G81 OTA built by Saxon Sandbech
(photo – Gary Chapman)

1991 Dennis RS237 Water Tender Ladder reg. no. H186 AFJ built
by JDC (photo – Gary Chapman)

1992 Volvo FL10 Aerial Ladder Platform reg. no. J869 MFJ built by
Angloco with Bronto Skylift 28-2TI booms (photo – Colin Dunford)

Iveco 140-25A chassis fitted with Magirus DLK30E ladders. When the older urban Dennis RS appliances became due for replacement three Dennis Rapier TF203 appliances were purchased in 1994 again bodied by JDC. The same year four Mercedes-Benz 1124F appliances with Carmichael bodies were delivered. Also in 1994 two appliances were built on the 4x4 Mercedes-Benz 917AF chassis to cope with the moorland requirements of stations like Princetown and Lynton. Twenty-four MAN 10/224F Compact Water Tenders built by Saxon-Sandbech were delivered between 1995 and 1996. A home designed appliance was built in 1996 by Devon's workshops on a Mercedes-Benz 814D 4x4 chassis for the volunteer station at Kingston. Four Prime Movers were purchased between 1995 and 1997 based on the MAN 18.224 chassis and fitted with Multilift hydraulically operated hook-lift systems. The first demountable pods purchased were two Breathing Apparatus Training Units and a Control Unit for use at large incidents. Once these were evaluated a decision was made to replace the service's Emergency Tenders with two new types of pods. The pods were supplied as a pair to selected stations together with a Prime Mover. The first was the Incident Support Unit (ISU) which carried lighting, portable generators, propping and shoring gear, salvage equipment, hi-expansion foam equipment, smoke extraction fans and additional BA cylinders. It also incorporated washing and

One of three Dennis Rapier TF203R3B Water Tender Ladders built by JDC and delivered in 1994 (photo – Gary Chapman)

1994 Mercedes 97AF 4 wheel drive Water Tender Ladder reg. no. M561 HOD built by Carmichael for use on Dartmoor
(photo – Gary Chapman)

Between 1995 and 1996 twenty-four MAN 10.224F Compact Water Tender Ladders were built by Saxon-Sandbech (photo – Gary Chapman)

1996 Mercedes-Benz 814D Light Pump reg. no. P933 ATT converted by Devon's workshops (photo – Gary Chapman)

MAN 18.224F Prime Mover reg. no. P391 ETT seen here loaded with one of the ISU pods (photo – Gary Chapman)

One of four Incident Command Vehicles based on the Mercedes-Benz Vito van (photo – Gary Chapman)

toilet facilities and a kitchen area for supplying hot meals and drinks. The other pod was the Environmental Unit which carried a wide range of absorbent materials, special protective clothing, containers for contaminated waste, vacuum units for removing hazardous powders, portable dam units for storing waste liquids, floating booms and decontamination equipment.

New Incident Command Vehicles (ICVs) were also needed to replace the Emergency Tender based vehicles and four were purchased in 1999 based on the Mercedes-Benz Vito van. As well as powerful computers and communications equipment each ICV carries an air supported structure, lighting and collapsible furniture to provide a command post/briefing room.

To meet the need for rescues in specialist areas such as from a height or confined space a Line Rescue Unit was formed at Camel's Head fire station in Plymouth and equipped with a Mercedes-Benz Unimog vehicle. When a second unit was formed at Barnstaple for the North Devon area it was supplied with a Land Rover vehicle. It 1996 Dennis Brothers had introduced the Sabre chassis and by 2001 JDC had delivered sixteen Water Tenders built on this chassis

The 1942 Plymouth fireboat *Cissie Brock* came to the end of its working life in the 1990s and was eventually replaced in 2000 by a new fireboat *Vigiles*. The aluminium catamaran hull was built by Alnmaritec of Northumberland and has a water jet propulsion system giving a service speed of 25 knots. The fire pump is powered by a separate diesel engine feeding a number of deliveries as well as monitor positions. At the stern of the craft is a water level rescue platform whilst the cabin has accommodation for the five man crew as well as stretcher borne casualties.

A new Aerial Ladder Platform was also delivered in 2000 built by Angloco on a MAN 18.284F chassis with Bronto F32MDT booms.   Four Foam/Water Carriers built on the MAN 18.284F 4x4 chassis by Massey Tankers were delivered in 2001 and to complement the service's foam capability an Iveco Cargo flat bed lorry was supplied fitted with a Hiab crane.   This vehicle carried 1,000 litre IBC Foam Containers and relevant equipment.   Two Hose Layers were purchased in 2003 and 2004 built by Fosters Commercials on the MAN 18.280 chassis and fitted with Angus Hose Retrieval Systems.   By 2006 forty-three more Water Tenders had been delivered by JDC built on various MAN chassis.   The one exception was a Dennis Dagger F98 delivered in 2002 by JDC.

In 2007 Devon and Somerset Fire and Rescue Services were amalgamated into one large combined authority.

Mercedes-Benz Unimog U20L Line Rescue Unit reg. no. V521 LFJ built by JDC in 2000 (photo – Gary Chapman)

One of sixteen Water Tender Ladders built by JDC on the Dennis Sabre chassis was reg. no. V624 ETT (photo – Graham Eglen)

Vigiles the Twin Hulled Fireboat built in 2000 by Alnmaritec (photo – Devon and Somerset Fire and Rescue Service)

This MAN 18.284F Aerial Ladder Platform reg. no. X916 BFJ built by Angloco with Bronto F32MDT booms was delivered in 2000 (photo – Gary Chapman)

This Foam Unit was based on a 2001 Iveco Cargo chassis reg. no. Y237 JPM (photo – Gary Chapman)

MAN 18.284F 4x4 Water/Foam Carrier reg. no. WA51 OOG one of four delivered in 2001 (photo – Gary Chapman)

2002 Dennis Dagger F28 Water Tender reg. no. WJ02 XOG built by JDC (photo – Graham Eglen)

One of a pair of Hose Layers operated by Devon was this 2003 MAN LE18.280 4x4 reg. no. WA03 VTE (photo – Gary Chapman)

2004 MAN 14.285 Water Tender Ladder reg. no. WA04 DHG built by JDC (photo – Graham Eglen)

Another JDC built Water Tender Ladder is this 4x4 version built on the MAN 10.220 chassis in 2006 (photo – Gary Chapman)

Somerset Fire Brigade 1948-1974

The brigade was formed in 1948 with forty-one fire stations but by 1970 fire stations at Milborne Port, Wedmore and Watchet had been closed. As with the rest of British brigades the fleet taken over from the NFS consisted of a mixture of pre-war and wartime appliances.

Appliances known to have to have been taken over by Somerset Fire Brigade in 1948

Built	Type	Chassis	Body	Reg. No.
1930	Pump Escape	Leyland Cub		BYC 145
1934	Pump	Dennis		BPB 644
1938	Towing Vehicle	Bedford		EYC 621
1940	Pump	Leyland Cub		EYD 586
1942	Pump Escape	Leyland		FYA 785
1942	Pump Escape	Leyland Tiger		FYC 412
1942	Hosereel Tender (1)	Austin K2		GGX 80
1942	Hosereel Tender (1)	Austin K2		GGX 149
1942	ATV & Trailer Pump	Austin K2		GGX 287
1942	Hosereel Tender (1)	Austin K2		GGX 426
1942	Hosereel Tender (1)	Austin K2		GGX 631
1942	ATV & Trailer Pump	Austin K2		GLE 142
1942	Hosereel Tender (1)	Austin K2		GLE 143
1942	ATV & Trailer Pump	Austin K2		GLE 146
1942	ATV & Trailer Pump	Austin K2		GLR 359
1942	ATV & Trailer Pump	Austin K2		GLR 493
1942	Emergency Tender (1)	Austin K2		GLR 494
1942	ATV & Trailer Pump	Austin K2		GLT 79
1942	ATV & Trailer Pump	Austin K2		GLT 80
1942	Control Unit (1)	Austin K2		GLT 338
1943	ATV & Trailer Pump	Austin K2		GXH 75
1943	ATV & Trailer Pump	Austin K2		GXH 184
1943	Hosereel Tender (1)	Austin K2		GXH 187
1943	Emergency Tender (1)	Austin K2		GXH 361
1943	ATV & Trailer Pump	Austin K2		GXH 364
1943	ATV & Trailer Pump	Austin K2		GXH 413
1943	Emergency Tender (1)	Austin K2		GXH 665
1943	ATV & Trailer Pump	Austin K2		GXH 666
1943	ATV & Trailer Pump	Austin K2		GXH 669
1943	ATV & Trailer Pump	Austin K2		GXH 672
1944	Water Tender (2)	Dodge		GXM 633
1944	Turntable Ladder	Austin K4	Merryweather 60 feet	GXN 205
1944	Turntable Ladder	Austin K4	Merryweather 60 feet	GXN 208
1944	Turntable Ladder	Austin K4	Merryweather 60 feet	GXN 218
1945	Water Tender A	Fordson WOT 6		GYR 223
1945	Water Tender A	Fordson WOT 6		GYR 223

(1)   Ex ATV
(2)   Ex Mobile Dam Unit

This immaculately preserved 1936 Leyland FK6 Pump Escape
reg. no. BYC 145 was originally purchased by the Borough of
Yeovil in Somerset (photo – Mike Williams)

1944 Austin K4 Turntable Ladder reg. no. GXN 205 built with
Merryweather 60 feet ladders, seen here in preservation
(The Roy Yeoman Collection)

It was in 1950 that the first new appliances were purchased when two Commer 21A Water
Tenders were built by Whitson. Also the same year a Dennis F7 Pump Escape and an AEC Regal
Turntable Ladder with Merryweather ladders were delivered. In 1951 six Dennis F12 Pump
Escapes and one Dennis F12 Pump were purchased along with eight more Commer Water
Tenders. By 1952 Alfred Miles & Sons had begun building fire appliances and supplied
Somerset with nine Water Tenders built on a mixture of the Commer 21A chassis and the
Commer 45A chassis. From 1955 to 1957 nine Dennis F25 Water Tenders were delivered
followed in 1959 by five Dennis F28 Water Tenders. Also during the 1950s a total of fourteen
Land Rover light vehicles had been purchased.

In 1960 Somerset obtained a Recovery Vehicle built locally on a Bedford RLHZ chassis. A
further five Dennis F28 Water Tenders were purchased in 1961 before Somerset changed to
Bedford based appliances with three Bedford TKG Water Tenders being built by Hampshire Car
Bodies (HCB) who also built a Foam Tender/Hose Layer in 1962 on a Bedford TKG chassis. In
1965 a Pump Hydraulic Platform was purchased built on a Bedford TKG chassis by

1950 AEC Regal Turntable Ladder reg. no. LYB 388 built with Merryweather 100 feet ladders (The Roy Yeoman Collection)

1954 Commer QX Water Tender Escape reg. no. WYA 559 built by Alfred Miles seen here in preservation (unknown photographer)

1959 Dennis F28 Water Tender reg. no. 20 FYD again seen in preservation (photo – Bob Smith)

1960 Bedford RLHZ Recovery Vehicle reg. no. 815 KYB
(photo – Colin Dunford)

1962 Bedford TKG Foam Tender/Hose Layer reg. no. 871 SYB
built by HCB (unknown photographer)

1968 Bedford TJ5 Water Tender reg. no. RYC 470F built by HCB-
Angus (The Colin Dunford Collection)

HCB and fitted with Simon SS65 booms. Between 1964 and 1969 HCB-Angus (HCB-A) built a total of fifteen Water Tenders on the Bedford TJ5 chassis and three on the TKG chassis. .

In 1970 Somerset purchased two Ford Transit Light Pumps (L2Ps) for use by the volunteer units at Banwell and Wrington to replace wartime ATVs and Trailer Pumps. Between 1970 and 1974 twenty-three Water Tenders were delivered by HCB-A built on the Bedford TKEL chassis. Two Pump Hydraulic Platforms were delivered in 1971 and 1973 built by HCB-A on the ERF 84PF chassis with Simon SS50 booms. Meanwhile in 1972 and 1974 two Rescue Tenders were built by HCB-A by converting Ford Transit vans.

This 1972 ERF 84PFS Hydraulic Platform reg. no. PCK 999K built by CFE with Simon SS70 booms was purchased second hand from Lancashire Fire Brigade (photo – Colin Dunford)

Banwell 1970 Ford Transit L2P reg. no. XYB 514H built by HCB-A (photo – Pete Ashpool)

One of twenty-three Water Tenders built in the early 1970s was this Bedford TKEL reg. no. PYC 322L (The Roy Yeoman Collection)

1973 ERF 84PFS Pump Hydraulic Platform reg. no. OYB 999L and fitted with Simon SS50 booms (photo – Mike Lawmon)

Somerset Fire Brigade 1974-1996

Following the 1974 Local Government Act fourteen fire stations from Somerset's "A" Division were transferred to the new Avon Fire Brigade bringing the total number of stations down to twenty-four; three wholetime/retained with the remainder retained crewed.

In 1974 a Range Rover six wheeled Light Pump was purchased from Carmichaels for use at Dulverton Fire Station on Exmoor, a Bedford TK Water Carrier was built by Wincanton Motors and two Ford Transits were fitted out by Somerset's workshops as Control Units. During the 1970s a total of sixteen Land Rovers were delivered, one for use as a Cliff Rescue Unit. Another Water Carrier was built by Wincanton Motors in 1976 on a Bedford TK chassis followed by seven Water Tenders built by Carmichael on the Dodge K1113 chassis. A further six were delivered in 1977, three built by HCB-A and three by Cheshire Fire Engineering (CFE). The next delivery of pumping appliances was between 1980 and 1981 when HCB-A delivered a total of eleven built on the Bedford TKG chassis. Meanwhile, in 1980, HCB-A had built a Road Accident Unit using a converted Ford Transit van. A Hose Layer/Foam/Salvage Tender was ordered from Wincantons in 1981 again built on a Bedford TKG chassis. Saxon became the preferred body supplier and delivered nine Water Tenders built on the Bedford TKG chassis between 1982 and 1984. Two new Control Units were delivered in 1983 again using Ford Transits fitted out by the brigade's workshops. Saxons delivered a Reynolds Boughton RB44 Rescue Tender in 1984 and two Incident Support Units in 1986 based on Rover Sherpa vans. Between 1986 and 1988 twelve Water Tenders were built by Saxon on the Dodge G13C chassis. In 1989 Mercedes-Benz appliances first appeared in Somerset's fleet when two Water Tenders were delivered by Saxons built on the 1120F chassis. Also that year two Hydraulic Platforms were built by Saxons on the Mercedes-Benz 1625-52 chassis fitted with Simon ST240 booms.

Saxons continued to build on various Mercedes-Benz chassis and in 1990 delivered a Water Carrier on a 1625-52 chassis and a Rescue Tender on a 711D chassis. Eight Water Tenders were built by Saxons on the Mercedes-Benz 1120F chassis between 1990 and 1991. Three 'special appliances' were delivered in 1991; a Water Carrier on a Mercedes 1722-45 chassis, a L6P on a Steyr Pinzgauer 718K chassis and a Control Unit on a Mercedes-Benz 814D chassis all built by Saxons. Also four Water Tenders were built by Saxons in 1991 all on the Mercedes-Benz 1120F chassis. When the upgraded Mercedes-Benz 1124F chassis became available in 1992 thirteen Water Tenders were built by Saxons and delivered by 1997. Another Steyr-Puch Pinzgauer L6P

1974 Range Rover Commando L6P reg. no. SYC 124L built by Carmichael (photo – Colin Dunford)

1976 Dodge K1113 Water Tender reg. no. PYC 762P also built by Carmichael (photo – Bob Smith)

was ordered from Saxons in 1994 followed in 1995 by a Hydraulic Platform built on a Mercedes-Benz 1824 chassis fitted with Simon SS263 booms. Replacement Land Rovers continued to be delivered with a total of twenty-six delivered by the turn of the century.

1980 Ford Transit 160 Road Accident Unit reg. no. KYC 876V built by HCB-Angus (The Colin Dunford Collection)

1981 Bedford TKG Hose Layer/Foam/Salvage Tender reg. no. YYA 833X built by Wincanton Motors (photo – Bob Smith)

1984 Bedford TKG Water Tender Ladder reg. no. B872 XYA built by Saxon (photo – Bob Smith)

1988 Dodge G13C Water Tender reg. no. E434 SYD built by Saxon (photo – Bob Smith)

1990 Mercedes-Benz LN1120 Water Tender Ladder reg. no. G481 LYC built by Saxon (photo – Colin Dunford)

1990 Mercedes-Benz 1625 Aerial Ladder Platform reg. no. G484 LYC built by Saxon with Simon ST240S booms (photo – Colin Dunford)

1992 Mercedes-Benz 1772-45 Water Carrier reg. no. J58 BYB built by Saxon (photo – Colin Dunford)

1994 Steyr-Puch Pinzgauer 718K Light Pump reg. no. L899 NYA built by Saxon (photo - Colin Dunford)

1995 Mercedes-Benz 1824 Hydraulic Platform reg. no. N826 BYC built by Saxon with Simon SS263 booms (photo - Colin Dunford)

Somerset Fire and Rescue Service 1996-2007

Somerset changed its title to the Somerset Fire and Rescue Service in 1996 reflecting its wider scope and in 1997 Saxons delivered two Incident Support Units built on the Mercedes-Benz 817 chassis followed by a Hose Layer/Foam/Salvage Tender built on a Mercedes-Benz 917 chassis in 1998. The brigade's workshops fitted out two Land Rover Defenders for use as Command Support Units in 1999 followed by the purchase of a Supacat 6x6 All Terrain Vehicle for use on Exmoor.

New appliances purchased in the first year of the new millennium included a Foam Carrier built by Saxons on a Mercedes-Benz 1324AF chassis and another Land Rover Command Support Unit. A major upgrade to the fleet occurred in 2000 with Saxons supplying twelve Water Tenders built on the Volvo FL6.14 chassis. When Saxons introduced the Volumax cab for the Volvo FL6.14 chassis Somerset ordered eight for delivery in 2002. The last Saxon built appliances were two Rescue Tenders delivered in 2003 built on the Mercedes-Benz chassis. With Saxons ceasing trading JDC won a contract to build pumping appliances and between 2004 and 2006 delivered eleven Water Tenders built on the MAN 14.280 chassis.

In 2007 Somerset Fire and Rescue Service amalgamated with Devon Fire and Rescue Service to form one single authority.

1997 Mercedes-Benz 817 Incident Support Unit reg. no. P96 JYC built by Saxon (photo – Bob Smith)

1997 Mercedes-Benz 1124F Water Tender Ladder reg. no. P894 KYD was one of thirteen built by Saxon (photo – Colin Dunford)

1998 Mercedes-Benz 917 Hose Layer/Foam/Salvage Tender reg. no. S796 WAY built by Saxons (photo – Colin Dunford)

1999 Land Rover Defender 110 Tdi Command Support Unit reg. no. T269 RYC (photo – Colin Dunford)

2000 Volvo FL6.14 Water Tender Ladder reg. no. W265 RYB built by Saxon with a Volumax cab (photo – Colin Carter)

One of a pair of Rescue Tenders delivered in 2003 was this Mercedes-Benz Atego 1328 built by Saxon (photo – Paul Morrey)

2005 MAN 13.285 Water Tender Ladder reg. no. WA05 DFN built by JDC (photo – Colin Carter)

Devon and Somerset Fire & Rescue Service 2007- onwards

The combined service is now the second largest Fire and Rescue Service in England and the largest non-metropolitan with eighty-five fire stations; six wholetime, eight wholetime/retained, one day-crewed/retained, two volunteer and the remainder retained. The service employs nearly 800 wholetime firefighters and 1,200 retained firefighters with 170 front-line fire appliances.

Two Water Carriers were the first appliances purchased by the new combined fire and rescue service built by The Vehicle Application Centre (TVAC), one on a MAN LE 18.280 chassis and the other on a MAN TGM 18.283 chassis. 2007 saw the commencement of a Co-responder scheme set up in conjunction with South West Ambulance Service. To aid this service a fleet of fourteen Vauxhall Corsa Combi vehicles were purchased by the ambulance service. Also in the year 2007, TVAC built a Rescue Tender on a MAN TGL 12.240 chassis. Between 2007 and 2009 JDC delivered sixteen Water Tenders on the MAN LE 14.280 chassis using PolyBilt bodies. Meanwhile in 2008 a Heavy Rescue Tender had been ordered from JDC again with a PolyBilt body on a MAN TGL 12.240 chassis.

Five Aerial Ladder Platforms were ordered in 2010 to be built by JDC on the MAN 23.360 6x2 chassis fitted with Vema booms. JDC continued to build Water Tenders for the fleet and

2008 MAN 12.240 Heavy Rescue Tender reg. no. WA08 HVB built by JDC with a PolyBilt body (photo – Bob Smith)

One of the fleet of Emergency Response Units used for Co-Responding is this 2008 Vauxhall Combo reg. no. KU58 ZDR (photo – Graham Eglen)

2010 MAN 23.360 Aerial Ladder Platform reg. no. WA59 FUB, one of five identical appliances, built by JDC and fitted with Vema booms (photo – Graham Eglen)

delivered seven more in 2010 built on the MAN TGL 12.240 chassis still with PolyBilt bodies. 2010 also saw the delivery of two JCB Groundhog All Terrain Vehicles for use on Exmoor. Also in 2010 a new concept was trialled with the delivery of a Light Rescue Pump (LRP) built by JDC on the Iveco Daily 65C18 chassis with PolyBilt bodywork. Four Special Rescue Tenders were the next additions to the fleet being built by JDC on the Iveco Daily 55S17W 4x4 chassis between 2010 and 2011. These Rescue Tenders combine the roles of line, water and animal rescue. Following the trial of the LRP a further two were purchased in 2011 built on the Mitsubishi Canter chassis by JDC and brigade workshops also built two between 2011 and 2012. Also in 2012 a Manitou MT932 Telehandler was purchased and based with the Special Operations team at Headquarters. In 2013 a large order was placed for eighteen Toyota HiLux 4x4 Light Pumps which were fitted with Strongs bodies by workshops. Also that year four Hazmat/Environmental Protection Units were fitted out by brigade workshops on the Mercedes-Benz Sprinter 519 van base. In 2014 a Water Rescue Unit was put on the run built on a Mercedes-Benz Sprinter van chassis and following the appraisal of the original Light Rescue Pumps six more were delivered in 2014 but this time built by Emergency-One on the Iveco Eurocargo chassis with a further sixteen being delivered in 2015.

One of a pair purchased for use on Exmoor is this 2010 JCB Ground Hog 4x4 All Terrain Vehicle reg. no. WA60 FCE towed by a Land Rover 110 reg. no. WA09 CZY
(photo – Colin Carter)

One of the original Light Rescue Pumps was this Iveco Daily 65C18 reg. no. WA60 FGD built by JDC
(photo – Mike Williams)

2010 Special Rescue Tender reg. no. WA60 FGF built by JDC on an Iveco Daily 55S17W 4x4 chassis with PolyBilt bodywork (photo – Mike Williams)

2013 Mercedes-Benz Sprinter 519 Hazmat/Environmental Protection Unit reg. no. WF13 XOZ (photo – Lester Solway)

2014 Mercedes-Benz Sprinter Water Rescue Unit reg. no. WX14 CYH (The Author's Collection)

One of the Mark 2 Light Rescue Pumps is this 2015 Iveco
Eurocargo reg. no. SF15 NGN built by Emergency-One
(photo – Lester Solway)

A line-up of some the Rapid Intervention Units at Service HQ
(photo – Devon and Somerset Fire and Rescue Service)

In 2015 a project was started to evaluate the introduction of Rapid Intervention Units (RIUs) into the fleet. The RIUs are smaller vehicles and an important element of the trial will be testing new types of equipment. Ten fire stations were selected for the pilot scheme, both wholetime and retained crewed. A range of vehicles have been converted which will be used for the trial including an Isuzu D-Max Yukon pickup, two Iveco Daily vans, two Mercedes-Benz Sprinter vans, a Toyota Hilux 3.5T pickup and two Volkswagen Transporter 3.2 ton vans and each will carry different firefighting equipment

Today the operational fleet consists of one hundred and sixteen various pumping appliances, eight Rapid Intervention Units, six Aerial Ladder Platforms, one Hydraulic Platform, six Water Carriers, four Rescue Tenders, four Special Rescue Tenders, one Water Rescue Unit, four Hazmat Units, two Incident Support Units, one Hose/Foam/Salvage Tender, thirty-eight Light 4-wheel drive Vehicles, two Light 6-wheel drive Pumps, six Incident Command Vehicles, two All Terrain Vehicles, six Inshore Rescue Boats, one Fireboat, eleven Prime Movers, two Operational Support pods, three Welfare pods, two Foam pods, one Incident Support pod, three Incident Response Units, two High Volume Pumping pods, two High Volume Hose Layer pods, five Urban Search and Rescue pods, one Mass Decontamination Dis-robe pod and one Mass Decontamination Re-robe pod.

Avon - 2008 MAN TG-M 18.280 Rescue Tender reg.no. WX58 FJN built by JDC with a PolyBilt body and fitted with a HIAB crane (photo – Colin Carter)

Avon operate two Combined Aerial Rescue Pumps one of which is this 2010 Scania P340 6x2 reg. no. KX10 EOY built by JDC with a PolyBilt body and fitted with Vema 282 booms. (photo – Colin Carter)

Cornwall – A typical retained fire station with a Mercedes-Benz Atego Water Tender Ladder and a Vauxhall Brava Light Pump (photo – Gary Chapman)

Cornwall - This 2010 Mercedes-Benz Atego 1329F Rescue Tender reg. no. WK10 DHO was built by JDC with a Polybilt body and operates out of Bodmin Fire Station
(photo – Gary Chapman)

Devon – 2002 MAN 12.225 Compact Water Tender Ladder reg. no. WJ52 ZZD built by JDC (photo – Gary Chapman)

Devon – Five Aerial Ladder Platforms were delivered in 2009 built on the MAN 23.360 chassis and fitted with Vema 343TFL booms by JDC. This one reg. no. WA59 FUF is stationed Crownhill Fire Station in Plymouth (photo – Mike Williams)

76

Dorset – 1977 Bedford TKG Water Tender reg. no. RRU 47R built by HCB-Angus
(photo – Colin Dunford)

Dorset – Scania P270 Water Tender Ladder reg. no. RX56 FKR built by Emergency One
in 2007 (photo – Gary Chapman)

Gloucestershire – 1967 Ford D600 Water Tender reg. no. KDF 454E built by HCB-Angus (photo – Mike Lawmon)

Gloucestershire – 1992 Dennis TF202 Rapier Water Tender Ladder reg. no. K283 SDF built by JDC (photo – Mike Lawmon)

Isles of Scilly - This 1981 Land Rover L4P reg.no. ECV 854V originally served with Cornwall Fire Brigade (The Gary Chapman Collection)

Isles of Scilly - 1997 Mercedes-Benz 1124AF Water Tender reg. no. P156 SCY built by Carmichaels is based on St. Mary's (The Gary Chapman Collection)

Somerset – 1987 Dodge G13 Water Tender reg.no. E433 SYD built by Saxons
(photo – Colin Dunford)

Somerset – One of two operated by Somerset Fire Brigade was this 1994 Steyr Puch
Pinzgauer 6x6 Light Pump reg. no. L899 NYA built by Saxons (photo – Colin Dunford)

80

Wiltshire – This 1951 Dennis Pump Escape reg. no. HMR 765 now preserved by Wiltshire Fire and Rescue Service (photo – Malcolm Thompson)

Wiltshire – 2002 Dennis Sabre ML243L532GS4 Water Tender Ladder reg. no. WV52 CGY built by JDC (photo – Malcolm Thompson)

CHAPTER 4
DORSET

Following de-nationalisation in 1948 there were two separate fire brigades in the county; Bournemouth Fire Brigade and Dorset County Fire Service. The County Service was renamed in 1954 and became the Dorset Fire Brigade and then following local government re-organisation the two brigades were amalgamated into one on the 1st April 1974. The final change was the renaming in 2003 to the Dorset Fire and Rescue Service.

Bournemouth Fire Brigade 1948-1974

After de-nationalisation the brigade was formed in 1948 with a full-time strength of 50 men, based at four fire stations.

Appliances known to have been taken over from the NFS by Bournemouth Fire Brigade

Built	Type	Chassis	Body	Reg. No.
1938	Pump Escape	Leyland SFT4A		EEL 582
1939	Turntable Ladder	Albion	Merryweather 105ft	FEL 623
1939	Pump Escape	Leyland FK6 Cub		FLJ 356
1940	Hose Layer (1)	Fordson 7v		GGN 847
1942	Heavy Unit	Bedford		FYH 350
1943	Heavy Unit	Austin K4		GLE 811
1943	Heavy Unit	Austin K4		GLE 835
1943	Salvage Tender (2)	Austin K2		GLT 961
1943	ATV	Austin K2		GXH 259
1943	Escape Carrying Unit	Fordson 7v		GXM 169

(1)   Later converted to an Emergency Tender
(2)   Ex ATV

The first post-war appliance purchased by the County Borough was a Dennis F12 Pump Escape in 1951 followed in 1952 by a Pump built by Merryweather on an AEC Regent 3 chassis. Two more new appliances were bought in the 1950s both on the AEC Mercury chassis; a Turntable Ladder with 100 feet Merryweather ladders in 1958 and in 1959 a Pump Escape built with Merryweather Marquis bodywork.

More replacement appliances arrived in the 1960s including three more Pump Escapes built on the AEC Mercury chassis with Merryweather Marquis bodywork. These were delivered in 1960, 1964 and 1966. The AEC Mercury chassis was used in 1963 for an Emergency/Salvage Tender but this time the bodywork was carried out by Hampshire Car Bodies (HCB). Three Commer Water Tenders were supplied; two in 1963 and one in 1965.

Bournemouth's 1939 Leyland FK6 Cub Pump Escape reg.
no. FLJ 356 (The Author's Collection)

Bournemouth's 1963 Merryweather Mercury Emergency/
Salvage Tender reg. no. 3982 RU built by HCB
(The Wardell Collection)

1964 Merryweather Marquis Pump Escape reg. no. 9682
RU built on an AEC Mercury chassis seen here after
conversion to a Water Tender Ladder
(The Roy Yeoman Collection)

This 1974 Dennis F108 Pump Escape reg. no. OEL 718M, seen here without its wheeled escape, was the last appliance purchased by Bournemouth Fire Brigade (photo – Colin Dunford)

The last appliances purchased by Bournemouth Fire Brigade were two Dennis F108 Pump Escapes delivered in 1971 and 1974.

Dorset County Fire Service 1948-1954

Following the transfer from the National Fire Service (NFS) to the new Dorset County Fire Service on the 1st April 1948 there were three wholetime/retained stations and eighteen retained stations.

Appliances known to have been taken over from the NFS by Dorset County Fire Service

Built	Type	Chassis	Body	Reg. No.
1936	Pump Escape	Leyland Cub FK7		JT 5199
1938	Pump	Leyland		JT 9120
1938	Pump Escape	Leyland Tiger FT4A		JT 9723
1939	Pump	Bedford MJZ		APR 679
1940	Hosereel Tender	Fordson 7v		APR 839
1940	Hosereel Tender	Fordson 7v		APR 840
1940	Pump	Fordson 7v		APR 876
1940	Pump Escape	Leyland FK8 Cub		APR 888
1941	Escape Carrying Unit	Fordson 7v		GGK 138
1941	Escape Carrying Unit	Fordson 7v		GGK 154
1942	Heavy Unit	Austin K4		GLE 845
1942	Heavy Unit	Austin K4		GLE 949
1942	ATV	Austin K2		GLR 77
1942	ATV	Austin K2		GLR 88
1943	Turntable Ladder	Leyland Beaver	Merryweather 100ft	GXA 62
1943	Turntable Ladder	Leyland Beaver	Merryweather 100ft	GXA 62
1943	Escape Carrying Unit	Austin K4		GXA 725
1943	ATV	Austin K2		GXH 336
1943	ATV	Austin K2		GXH 338
1943	ATV	Austin K2		GXH 399
1944	Water Tender (1)	Fordson 7v		GXM 278
1944	Water Tender (1)	Dodge		GXM 555

Built	Type	Chassis	Body	Reg. No.
1944	Water Tender (1)	Dodge		GXM 557
1944	Water Tender (1)	Dodge		GXO 533

(1)   Converted from Mobile Dam Units

The first post-war appliance purchased by the new brigade, a Dennis F12 Pump Escape delivered in 1952, was to become the only Dennis appliance in the fleet. Between 1953 and 1954 five Water Tenders and three Water Tender Escapes were built by HCB all on the Bedford SLZ chassis.

Dorset Fire Brigade 1954-1974

In 1954 the brigade was renamed the Dorset Fire Brigade and between 1955 and 1963 seven Water Tenders were built on the Karrier Gamecock chassis by Carmichaels.

During the period from 1956 through to 1964 HCB delivered eleven Water Tenders; one built on the Bedford SLZ chassis, one on the Bedford D4 chassis with the remainder built on the

1938 Leyland Tiger FT4A Pump Escape reg. no. JT 9723 which was in service pre-war with Poole Fire Brigade (photo – Ken Davis)

1961 Karrier Gamecock 72A Water Tender reg. no. UFX 157 built by Carmichaels (photo – Ken Davis)

Bedford TJ4L chassis.

In 1960 Dorset's workshops began fitting out Land Rovers for use as Light 4x4 Tenders and by 1974 had completed a total of thirty-three vehicles. Also in 1964 two Commer KC40 Walkthru vans were converted by workshops for use as Emergency Tenders. By 1965 HCB had become HCB-Angus (HCB-A) and continued to supply Bedford TJ4L Water Tenders delivering a further twelve by 1969. Following the demise of the Auxiliary Fire Service (AFS) in 1968 Dorset obtained four Bedford SHZ Emergency Pumps and a Bedford SLZ Control Unit.

1970 saw the introduction of the Bedford TKEL appliances into the fleet when HCB-A delivered two Water Tenders, one Water Tender Ladder and one Water Tender Escape. The wartime Turntable Ladders were replaced in 1972 with two Merryweather appliances built on the AEC Mercury 7 Ergomatic chassis. Also that year a Foam Carrier and a Canteen Van were delivered built by Hawson on the Bedford TJ chassis. HCB-A continued to supply pumping appliances delivering nine Water Tenders between 1972 and 1974 all built on the Bedford TKG chassis.

One of a pair delivered in 1972 to Dorset Fire Brigade was this AEC Mercury 7 Turntable Ladder reg. no. PPR 813K fitted with Merryweather 100 ft. ladders (The Graham Eglen Collection)

This 1972 Dennis D Water Tender Ladder reg. no. GHO 897K was taken over in 1974 by Dorset Fire Brigade along with Christchurch Fire Station (photo – Colin Dunford)

Dorset Fire Brigade 1974-2003

When local government was reorganised in 1974 the Bournemouth Borough Fire Brigade with its four wholetime fire stations and the retained station of Christchurch, formerly part of Hampshire Fire Brigade merged with the county brigade to form the new Dorset Fire Brigade.

The new brigade continued to purchase Water Tenders built by HCB-A on the Bedford TKG chassis with eighteen delivered between 1976 and 1979. However in 1978 Cheshire Fire Engineering (CFE) had supplied a batch of three Water Tenders still built on the Bedford TKG chassis. Meanwhile in 1976 two Emergency Tenders had been purchased with Cocker bodywork on the same Bedford chassis and in 1977 Dorset's workshops had converted a Leyland Clydesdale milk tanker into a Water Carrier. By 1979 workshops had also fitted out a further eleven Land Rovers.

From 1980 until the demise of Bedford Trucks in 1985 HCB-A delivered a further sixteen Water Tenders on the TKG chassis and three on the TL1260 chassis. A new Hydraulic Platform was delivered in 1982 built with Simon SS263 booms on a Dennis F123 chassis. In 1982 the old ex-AFS Control Unit was replaced with a new appliance built on the Dodge S56 chassis. Two Foam Carriers were built by Locomotors; the first built on a Dodge S56 chassis and delivered in 1983 and the other delivered in 1984 but this time built on the Dodge S75 chassis. A new type of appliance was introduced into the fleet in 1986 with the delivery of two Breathing Apparatus Tenders built by Spectra on the Leyland Roadrunner 6-12 chassis. 1988 saw the delivery of the first Volvo appliance; a Hydraulic Platform built on a FL6.16 chassis and fitted with the booms

One of a pair delivered in 1976 was this Bedford TKG Emergency Tender reg. no. LEL 357P built by Cockers (unknown photographer)

1977 Leyland Clydesdale Water Carrier reg. no. RYA 679R converted by Dorset's workshops from a milk tanker (photo – Colin Dunford)

Bedford TKG Water Tender reg. no. WRU 573S was one of three built by CFE in 1978 (photo – Colin Dunford)

1979 Land Rover 109 Light Fire Tender reg. no. CJT 162T was one of many converted by Dorset's workshops (photo – Colin Dunford)

1982 Dennis F123 Hydraulic Platform reg. no. RLJ 999X fitted with Simon SS263 booms (unknown photographer)

1982 Dodge S56 Control Unit reg. no. WJT 651X built by Corvesgate (photo – Ken Davis)

1983 Bedford TKG Water Tender Ladder reg. no. BPR 180Y built by HCB-A (photo – Colin Dunford)

1984 Dodge S75 Foam Carrier reg. no. A108 NEL built by Locomotors (photo – Colin Dunford)

1986 Leyland Roadrunner 6-12 Breathing Apparatus Tender reg. no. C523 YRU built by Spectra (photo - Ken Davis)

from the 1982 vehicle. In 1987 two Land Rover 110 6x6 Light Rescue Units were built by Fire Safety Equipment. Between 1988 and 1989 HCB-A delivered seven Water Tenders all built on the Volvo FL6.14 chassis and during the same period supplied three Light Pumps built on the Land Rover 110 6x6 chassis. In 1989 the brigade purchased an ex-demonstrator Pump built by HCB-A on the Mercedes-Benz LN917AF 4x4 chassis.

In 1991 a new Hydraulic Platform was built by Saxons on a Volvo FL6.17 chassis using Simon ST240S booms and between 1990 and 1994 HCB-A delivered seventeen more Water Tenders built on the Volvo FL6.14 chassis. Also during the same period Dorset's workshops fitted out a further eleven Light 4x4 Tenders built on the Land Rover 110 chassis. In 1992 the brigade purchased a second-hand Rescue Tender from South Glamorgan Fire Service built on a Dodge S56 chassis. A new Water Carrier was purchased in 1993 built by Reynolds Boughton on a Volvo FL6.18 chassis. Following the success of the ex-demonstrator Mercedes-Benz appliance a further two Water Tenders were built by HCB-A on the LN917AF chassis in 1993. Two Breathing Apparatus Tenders were built by Spectra on the Leyland Daf 45-130 chassis and delivered in 1993 and 1994. The last Volvo FL6.14 Water Tenders were delivered in 1995 when

1988 Volvo FL6.16 Hydraulic Platform reg. no. E50 MEL fitted with Simon SS263 booms (The Graham Eglen Collection)

1989 Volvo FL6.14 Water Tender Ladder reg. no. F154 XFX built by HCB-Angus (photo – Colin Dunford)

One of a trio of Land Rover 110 6x6 Light Pumps built by HCB-Angus was reg. no. F338 VFX (photo – Colin Dunford)

1989 Mercedes-Benz LN917 4x4 Pump reg. no. F388 NLC built by HCB-Angus (The Graham Eglen Collection)

1991 Volvo FL6.17 Aerial Ladder Platform reg. no. G220 FFX was built by Saxon and fitted with Simon ST240S booms (photo – Colin Dunford)

1993 Volvo FL6-18 Water Carrier reg. no. K907 VRU built by Reynolds Boughton (photo – Ken Davis)

1993 Leyland Daf 45-130 Breathing Apparatus Tender reg. no. L728 BFX built by Spectra (photo – Gary Chapman)

Saxons built three.   In 1996 a contract was signed with John Dennis Coachbuilders (JDC) for the supply of Dennis Sabre Water Tenders and by 1998 sixteen had been delivered. Also in 1996 three Operational Support Units based on the Ford Transit van chassis had been delivered and fitted out by workshops. Another Operational Support Unit was delivered in 1999 but this time built on an Iveco Daily chassis.

The new Millennium saw the continuation of the JDC contract and a further thirteen Dennis Sabre Water Tenders and four Land Rover Light 4x4 Tenders were delivered by 2002. Meanwhile two Aerial Ladder Platforms were built by Angloco in 2000; one on the Volvo FM12 chassis and the other on a MAN 18.284f chassis both with Bronto F32HDT 106 feet booms. Also delivered in 2000 was an Incident Command Unit built by Sortimo on a Mercedes-Benz 814D chassis. The first Scania appliance appeared in the fleet in 2001 when an Incident Support Unit, fitted with a Kooi Forklift Truck, was delivered with a Curtainsider body. Two Operational Support Units were delivered in 2002 built on the Mercedes-Benz Sprinter 814D chassis.

2000 Land Rover 110 4x4 Light Tender reg. no. V625 LYA built by JDC (photo – Gary Chapman)

2000 Volvo FM12 Aerial Ladder Platform reg. no. W296 AKM built by Angloco with Bronto F32HDT 106 feet booms (photo – Gary Chapman)

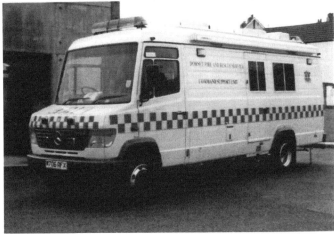

Sortimo built this 2000 Mercedes-Benz 814D Command Support Unit reg. no. W706 RFX (photo – Colin Dunford)

2001 Scania P94D-260 Incident Support Unit reg. no. Y654 KAN built with a Curtainsider body and carrying a Kooi Aap Forklift Truck (photo – Gary Chapman)

One of a pair of Operational Support Units is this 2002 Mercedes-Benz Sprinter 814D reg. no. HJ02 SXD (photo – Gary Chapman)

Five Dennis Sabre SFD253 Water Tender Ladders, including reg.
no. HJ02 XNY, were built in 2002 by JDC (photo – Graham Eglen)

2003 Iveco Welfare Support Unit reg. no. GN53 ZVO
(photo – Ken Davis)

Dorset Fire and Rescue Service 2003 – onwards

To reflect the wide role performed by the fire brigade it was renamed Dorset Fire and Rescue Service in 2003.

Three Environmental Support Units were built by between 2003 and 2004; two on the Mercedes-Benz Sprinter 814D chassis and one on the Renault Master LM35 chassis. A 2003 second-hand Iveco chassis was converted into a Welfare Unit providing hot drinks and snacks for crews plus toilet facilities. Then in 2004 there was a major change in the fleet when Scania became the preferred chassis and JDC built ten Water Tenders on the P94D-260 chassis. There were no further changes to the operational fleet until 2007 when Emergency One (E-One) delivered four Water Tenders built on the Scania P270 chassis. E-One then delivered another three identical Water Tenders in 2008 plus a 4-wheeled drive Water Tender built on a MAN TGM 13.240 chassis. Brigade workshops fitted out two Special Rescue Tenders; one built in 2008 on a Mercedes-Benz 814D chassis and the other in 2009 on a Nissan Navara 4x4 chassis. A Multi-Role Vehicle was built and delivered in 2009 by E-One based on a Mercedes-Benz Unimog U500 chassis. This was designed principally to deal with off-road heath fires and is fitted with a roof-top monitor.

2004 Scania P94D-260 Water Tender Ladder reg. no. RX04 FTF built by JDC (photo – Graham Eglen)

2008 MAN 4x4 Water Tender reg. no. HF57 AXJ reg. no. HF57 AXJ built by Emergency One (photo – Gary Chapman)

2009 Mercedes-Benz Unimog U500 4x4 Multi-Role Vehicle reg. no. AE09 HWB built by Emergency One (photo – Ken Davis)

2012 MAN TGL 12.250 Breathing Apparatus Tender reg. no. WN62 AWC built by Emergency One (photo – Ken Davis)

Over the next two years a further ten Water Tenders were delivered by E-One; six built on the Scania P270 chassis and four built on the MAN TGM 13.290 4x4 chassis. Two new Breathing Apparatus Tenders were delivered in 2012 built on the MAN TGL 12.250 chassis by E-One. Between 2014 and 2015 a further four MAN TGM 13.290 4x4 Water Tenders were built and delivered by E-One.

Today Dorset Fire and Service has three wholetime stations (all in Bournemouth), three wholetime/retained, one day crewed/retained and nineteen retained fire stations and has over 800 staff. The appliance fleet consists of thirty-two Water Tender Ladders, eight 4x4 Water Tenders, two Aerial Ladder Platforms, five Land Rover Light Pumps, seven Land Rover Light Tenders, one Unimog Multi-Role Vehicle, two Breathing Apparatus Support Units, one Command Support Unit, one Environmental Support Unit, one Incident Support Unit, one Welfare Unit, three Technical Rescue Units, one Animal Rescue Unit, one Incident Response Unit, four Prime Movers, three Water Carrier pods, one High Volume Pumping Unit pod, one High Volume Hose Laying Unit pod, one Mass Decontamination Dis-robe pod and one Mass Decontamination Re-robe pod.

Plans have been agreed to form a combined Fire Authority with Wiltshire Fire and Rescue Service with a single Fire and Rescue Service commencing 1st April 2016 with the joint Command and Control Centre based at Potterne, Wiltshire. The new joint service will be named the Dorset and Wiltshire Fire and Rescue Service with its headquarters in Salisbury, Wiltshire.

CHAPTER 5
GLOUCESTERSHIRE

When the fire service was de-nationalised in 1948 Gloucestershire had two fire brigades; the City of Gloucester Fire Brigade which covered the city and Gloucestershire Fire Service covering the remainder of the county. Following the major local government re-organisation on the 1st April 1974 the two brigades were amalgamated into one but at the same time four fire stations in the south of the county were transferred into the newly formed Avon Fire Brigade.

City of Gloucester Fire Brigade 1948-1974
Fire Appliances known to have been taken over from the National Fire Service

Built	Type	Chassis	Body	Reg. No.
1933	Pump Escape	Dennis Big 6		FH 8150
1938	Turntable Ladder	Leyland TLM	Metz 120ft	BFH 972
1941	Water Tender	Austin K4		
1941	Pump	Albion	Merryweather	
1941	Pump Escape (1)	Fordson 7v		
1942	Emergency Tender (2)	Austin K2		
1942	Foam Carrier (2)	Austin K2		
1942	Pump	Fordson 7v		GLW 166
1942	Salvage Tender (2)	Austin K2		GXH 682

(1)   Fitted with Barton front-mounted pump
(2)   Ex ATV

1952 HMI Annual Inspection of City of Gloucester Fire Brigade at Barnwood Road Fire Station. Appliances include (l to r) Leyland TLM Turntable Ladder, Dennis Big 6 Pump Escape, Fordson 7v Pump Escape and two Austin K2 ATVs. (The Clive Shearman Collection)

The City Brigade was formed in 1948 with a full-time strength of 50 men, based at two fire stations; Bearland and Barnwood Road until a new fire station, built in Eastern Avenue, was opened in 1956. A Dennis F7 Pump Escape was the first post-war appliance purchased by the city brigade in 1950 followed in 1952 by another Pump Escape this time a Dennis F12. No more appliances were purchased until 1958 when a Water Tender was supplied by Alfred Miles on a Bedford TJ4 chassis. A new Emergency Tender/Control Unit was purchased in 1964 built on a Bedford TKEL chassis with Dennis M bodywork to replace the ageing wartime ATV. To replace the pre-war Leyland Turntable Ladder a Hydraulic Platform was supplied in 1968 by HCB-Angus (HCB-A) built on an ERF 84RS chassis with Simon SS85 booms. In 1969 HCB-A also supplied the next appliance, a Ford D600 Water Tender.

The final appliances purchased by the city brigade arrived in 1972, a Dennis DJ Water Tender Ladder and a Ford D800 Pump Escape built by Pyrene. In 1974 the city brigade was amalgamated with the Gloucestershire Fire Service.

1964 Bedford TKEL Emergency Tender/Control Unit reg. no. 916 DFH built with Dennis M bodywork (The Author's Collection)

1972 Ford D800 Pump Escape reg. no. FFH 960K built by Pyrene (photo – Mike Lawmon)

This 1972 Dennis DJ Water Tender Ladder reg. no. JFH 958K built by Dennis Bros. was the last appliance purchased by the City Brigade (photo – Bob Smith)

Gloucestershire Fire Service 1948-1974

The new Gloucestershire Fire Service formed on the 1st April 1948 was based with its headquarters at Cheltenham. A full list of appliances taken over from the National Fire Service could not be traced but the table below shows the known vehicles.

Fire Appliances known to have been taken over from the National Fire Service

Built	Type	Chassis	Body	Reg. No.
1933	Pump	Dennis Braidwood		DG 8666
	Pump	Morris		CDG 303
1938	Pump Escape	Leyland FT4A		EAD 42
1943	Turntable Ladder	Leyland TSC44 Beaver	Merryweather 100ft	GXA 74
1943	ATV	Austin K2		GXH 682
1943	Breakdown Lorry	Bedford QL		GYR 145

The initial order placed post-war was in 1951 for three Water Tenders built on the Commer QX chassis with Alfred Miles bodywork and by 1959 a further twenty-two similar built appliances had been delivered; nineteen as Water Tenders, two as Pump Escapes and one as a Pump/Salvage Tender. The only other appliances purchased during the 1950s were a Dennis F12 Pump Escape in 1955, a Bedford RLHC Water Carrier in 1958, a Morris LD van in 1958 used as a Hosereel Tender and a Land Rover in 1959 used as a Lighting Unit.

Between 1960 and 1962 Alfred Miles built a further six Water Tender Escapes and one Water Tender still using the Commer QX chassis. 1960 also saw the introduction of smaller vehicles into the fleet when Carmichaels supplied seven Pumps on the Bedford J2 chassis with Hawson van conversions. A Rescue Vehicle was delivered in 1962 built by Miles on a Bedford RL chassis. The first new aerial appliance for the fleet, a Hydraulic Platform built by Hampshire Car Bodies (HCB) on an AEC Mercury chassis with Simon SS65 booms, arrived in 1964 to replace the wartime Turntable Ladder. Pyrene built a Foam Tender in 1965 on a Commer VAC chassis. The Commer VA6 chassis had replaced the QX chassis and eleven Water Tenders were delivered

This 1938 Leyland Pump Escape reg. no. EAD 42 was one of
the pre-war appliances taken over by Gloucestershire Fire
Service in 1948 (Unknown photographer)

1955 Dennis F12 Pump Escape reg. no. LAD 692
(photo – Mike Lawmon)

1957 Commer QX Water Tender reg. no. NDG 690 built by
Alfred Miles (photo – Mike Lawmon)

One of seven delivered in 1960 was this Bedford TJ2 Pump built by Carmichaels using a Hawson van conversion reg. no. 1600 AD (photo – Bob Smith)

1964 AEC Mercury Hydraulic Platform reg. no. BAD 659B built by HCB with Simon SS65 booms (The Author's Collection)

1966 Commer VA6 Water Tender reg. no. JDF 234D built with Dennis M bodywork (The Author's Collection)

1967 AEC Emergency Recovery Appliance reg. no. KDF 146E built by Marshalls and fitted with a Dial-Holmes crane (photo – Mike Lawmon)

1969 Ford D600 Water Tender reg. no. PDF 923G built by HCB-Angus (photo – Bob Smith)

1968 ERF 84RS Hydraulic Platform reg. no. MDD 747F built by HCB-Angus and fitted with Simon SS70 booms (photo – Mike Lawmon)

1973 Ford D1013 Pump Escape reg. no. DOD 700L built by HCB-Angus
(The Author's Collection)

using this chassis with Dennis M bodywork between 1965 and 1966. A Land Rover was purchased in 1967 which was used for towing a Hi-Expansion Foam Unit trailer. Also in 1967 a Foam Tender was built by HCB-Angus (HCB-A) on a Ford D600 chassis and an Emergency Recovery Appliance was also delivered built on an AEC chassis by Marshalls and fitted with a Dial-Holmes crane. In 1968 a new Hydraulic Platform was delivered by HCB-A built on an ERF 84RS chassis using Simon SS70 booms. Also in 1968 the Ford D600 chassis was introduced and HCB-A built eight Water Tenders, seven Water Tender Ladders and one Foam Tender all on this chassis by 1969.

HCB-A continued to supply Water Tenders with five built on the Ford D600 chassis in 1971 and twelve built on the Ford D1013 chassis between 1972 and 1973. Two Pump Escapes were also built by HCB-A in 1973 still using the Ford D1013 chassis.

Gloucestershire Fire Service 1974-1982

With the re-organisation of local government on April 1st 1974 four fire stations were transferred to the newly formed Avon Fire Brigade whilst the remainder of the County Fire Service and the City Fire Brigade were amalgamated into the new Gloucestershire Fire Service.

Five new Water Tenders were delivered in 1974 built on the Ford D1011 chassis by HCB-A. In 1975 four 'special appliances' were purchased; a new Emergency Recovery Vehicle built on a Ford DT2417 chassis and fitted with a Dial-Holmes crane, a Control Unit/Canteen Van built on a Ford A0610 chassis, a Land Rover Lighting Unit and another Land Rover which towed a Cliff

1975 Ford DT2417 Emergency Recovery Appliance reg. no. GDG 559N built by Bates and fitted with a Dial-Holmes crane
(photo – Mike Lawmon)

1975 Ford A0610 Control Unit/Canteen Van reg. no. HFN 671N built by Hawson (photo – Bob Smith)

1978 Bedford TKG Water Tender reg. no. VDF 864S built by Merryweather (photo – Bob Smith)

Hawsons fitted out this 1980 Ford A0610 Salvage Tender reg. no. GFH 951V
(The Author's Collection)

Bedford TKG Water Tender Ladder reg. no. JFH 318V built by Cheshire Fire Engineering, one of four supplied in 1980
(photo – Mike Lawmon)

Rescue Trailer. It was not until 1978 that the next batch of Water Tenders were delivered when six were built by Merryweather on the Bedford TKG chassis. A Foam Carrier was built in 1979 on a Ford A0610 chassis which also towed a Chemical Incident Unit trailer. The same year Cheshire Fire Engineering (CFE) delivered three Water Tender Ladders all built on the Bedford TKG chassis.

The last Bedford appliances for the fleet were delivered in 1980 when CFE built four more Water Tenders on the TKG chassis. A Ford A0610 Salvage Tender was fitted out by Hawsons and delivered in 1980 which also towed a Breathing Apparatus Tender trailer.

Gloucestershire Fire & Rescue Service 1982 - onwards

The service was renamed the Gloucestershire Fire and Rescue Service in 1982 to reflect the wider role of the modern service.

A Rescue Tender was built that year by Carmichaels on a Dodge S66 chassis and in 1983 Carmichaels built a Hazard Materials Unit on a Dodge G75 chassis. Two new aerial appliances were built by Carmichaels; in 1983 a Turntable Ladder on a Dodge G13 chassis with French Riffaud ladders and in 1984 a Hydraulic Platform on a Dodge G16 chassis using the booms from the old 1968 appliance. Carmichaels became the preferred bodybuilder delivering nineteen Water Tenders built on the Dodge G13 chassis between 1983 and 1986. The Dodge S56 chassis was used by Carmichaels in 1984 to build an Emergency Rescue Appliance. A new concept was designed in 1987, the Rapid Intervention Pump using the GMC K30 chassis. Two were built and delivered by Carmichaels, one of which was later converted to a Rescue Tender and a further four were delivered in 1988 before Telehoist supplied five in 1989. Fulton & Wylie, a Scottish body building company, appeared briefly on the scene delivering six Water Tenders built on the Leyland DAF 16-17 chassis between 1988 and 1989. A Turntable Ladder was delivered built in

1982 Dodge S66 Rescue Tender reg. no. JHY 616K built by Carmichael (photo – Mike Lawmon)

1984 Dodge G16L Hydraulic Platform reg. no. A796 FDG built by Carmichaels with Simon SS70 booms (photo – Colin Dunford)

1985 Dodge G13 Water Tender Ladder reg. no. B538 NDF built by Carmichaels (photo – Colin Dunford)

1987 GMC K30 Rapid Intervention Pump reg. no. D272 BFH built by Carmichaels (photo – Colin Dunford)

1988 by Carmichaels on an Iveco 140-25 chassis with Magirus ladders to replace the Riffaud ladders. Also in 1989 two Bedford Water Tenders were converted to Prime Movers and used in conjunction with a series of new Pods which included a Control Unit, a Damage Control Unit, an Incident Support Unit and a Display Unit.

The last Dodge based Water Tender was delivered in 1990 built by Rosenbauer on a G13 chassis. Other deliveries in 1990 were a Leyland DAF 2500 FAS Aerial Ladder Platform built by Angloco with Bronto 28-2TI booms and a Rescue Tender built by Rosenbauer on a Leyland 17-18 chassis and fitted with a HIAB crane. 1991 saw the introduction of Compact Water Tenders for use by the retained fire stations and four were delivered by Angloco with Rosenbauer bodywork built on the Leyland DAF 10-15 chassis. In 1992 three Land Rovers were delivered; two for use as Cliff Rescue Units and the other for towing an Inshore Rescue Boat. The supply of standard Water Tenders for the wholetime stations had seen a change with the introduction of the Dennis Rapier TF202 chassis and four were built by John Dennis Coachbuilders (JDC) between 1992 and 1993. Between 1992 and 1994 seven more Compact Water Tenders were delivered; four built by Locomotors and three by Carmichaels all on the Leyland DAF 45-160 chassis. The supply of Compact Water Tenders continued throughout the decade on the upgraded Leyland DAF 45-180 chassis with Carmichaels delivering four in 1995, Excalibur delivering two in 1996, two again in 1997 and JDC delivering two in 1999. Meanwhile in 1995 a Foam Support Unit was built by W. H. Bence and a new Water Carrier had been built by Massey Tankers on a Leyland DAF T60-210 chassis. By 1996 the Dennis Rapier had been superseded by the Sabre TSD233 chassis and JDC

1988 Leyland 16-17 Water Tender Ladder reg. no. E508 JFH built by Fulton & Wylie (photo – Colin Dunford)

1988 Iveco 140-25 Turntable Ladder reg. no. E368 LFW built by Carmichaels with Magirus ladders (photo – Mike Lawmon)

1990 Leyland DAF 2500 FAS Aerial Ladder Platform reg. no. G504 XFH built by Angloco and fitted with Bronto Skylift 28-2TI booms (photo – Colin Dunford)

1990 Leyland-DAF 17-18 Rescue Tender reg. no. G505 XFH built by Rosenbauer and fitted with a HIAB crane (photo – Colin Dunford)

1991 Leyland 10-15 Compact Water Tender Ladder reg. no. H737 JDG built by Angloco (photo – Bob Smith)

1992 Dennis Rapier TF202 Water Tender Ladder reg. no. K283 SDF built by John Dennis Coachbuilders (photo – Colin Dunford)

1993 Mercedes-Benz 1120 Rescue Tender reg. no. K938 UDF built by Locomotors (photo – Colin Dunford)

This Dodge G13 Prime Mover reg. no. A210 HFH was converted in 1994 from a Water Tender and is seen here loaded with the Incident Control Unit pod (photo – Mike Lawmon)

1995 Leyland DAF FA45-180Ti Compact Water Tender Ladder reg. no. N812 MFH built by Carmichael (photo – Colin Dunford)

1995 Leyland DAF FA45-180Ti Foam Support Unit reg. no. N814 MFH built by W. H. Bence (photo – Colin Dunford)

delivered six Water Tenders by 1998. Gloucestershire's workshops staff were busy in 1998 fitting out a Breathing Apparatus Support Unit on a Mercedes Benz Sprinter 412D chassis and four Light Tenders; two each on Vauxhall Brava 4x4's and Mitsubishi L2000 4x4 vehicles. MAN appliances were introduced into the fleet in 1999 when JDC built four Compact Water Tenders on the 10-224 chassis and two Rescue Tenders on the 18-264 chassis both fitted with HIAB cranes.

1995 Leyland-Daf T60-210 Water Carrier reg. no. N815 MFH built
by Massey Tankers (photo – Colin Dunford)

1998 Vauxhall Brava 4x4 Light Tender reg. no. R224 KDG built by
Gloucestershire's workshops (The Author's Collection)

The new millennium saw an Incident Command Unit built on a Dennis Dart SLF chassis and a one-off delivery of a Mercedes- Benz Atego Water Tender built by JDC. Six more Compact Water Tenders were also delivered between 2000 and 2002 by JDC all built on the MAN 10-224 chassis. In 2002 a Damage Control Unit was fitted out by the brigade's workshops on a Mercedes-Benz Sprinter chassis. Also in 2002 a Special Rescue Unit was built by JDC which was identical to the two Rescue Tenders delivered in 1999 and a new Aerial Ladder Platform was built by Saxon on a MAN 18.264 chassis with Magirus A320L booms. In 2003 the MAN chassis was upgraded and JDC delivered five Compact Water Tenders on the 12.224 chassis and four Land Rover vehicles were purchased. JDC also continued to supply Water Tenders delivering nine between 2002 and 2006 on the Dennis Sabre XL chassis. In 2005 an Environmental Protection Unit was built by A. G. Bracey of Bristol on a MAN 10.224 chassis. New appliances in 2007 consisted of a Breathing Apparatus Support Unit built on a Mercedes-Benz Sprinter chassis, an Aerial Ladder Platform built by Angloco on a MAN 18.264 chassis with Bronto 28-2Ti booms and a MAN 18.264 Foam and Water Carrier built by TVAC.

2000 Dennis Dart SLF222 Incident Command Unit reg. no. X771 ADG built by East Lancs. Coachbuilders (photo – Steve Dodge)

2000 Mercedes Benz Atego Water Tender Ladder reg. no. W918 VDD built by JDC (photo – Steve Dodge)

Gloucestershire's workshops fitted out this 2002 Mercedes-Benz Sprinter reg. no. VU51 BRX as a Damage Control Unit (photo – Steve Dodge)

2002 MAN TGL 18-264 Special Rescue Unit reg. no. VA02 NNC built by JDC and fitted with a HIAB crane (photo – Mike Williams)

2002 MAN 18.264f Aerial Ladder Platform reg. no. VU52 WNZ built by Saxons with Magirus A320L booms (The Author's Collection)

2003 Land Rover Defender 110 Light Vehicle reg. no. VU03 YFB used for towing a Rescue Boat (The Author's Collection)

2005 MAN LE 10.224 Environmental Protection Unit reg. no. VX55 NHF built by A. G. Bracey and fitted with sliding body doors (photo – Mike Williams)

2006 Dennis Sabre XL SFD322 Water Tender Ladder reg. no. VX56 PKN built by JDC (photo – Mike Williams)

2007 MAN TGL 18.264 Aerial Ladder Platform reg. no. VX07 NDD built by Angloco and fitted with Bronto 28-2Ti booms (photo – Mike Williams)

2007 MAN TGA 18.264 Foam and Water Carrier reg. no. VX07 OYV built by TVAC (photo – Mike Williams)

2008 MAN TGL 12-240 Water Tender Ladder reg. no. VX08 MKZ built by JDC (photo – Steve Dodge)

2010 Scania P270 Rescue Pump reg. no. KX10 EEJ built by Emergency One (photo – Mike Williams)

Between 2007 and 2009 seven Nissan Navara 4x4 towing vehicles were delivered. Nine Compact Waters were built by JDC on the MAN TGL 12.240 chassis and delivered between 2008 and 2010.

The first two Scania Water Tenders were built by Emergency One on the P270 chassis and delivered in 2011 followed later that year by a similar appliance built by JDC. In 2013 three more Water Tenders, now designated as Rescue Pumps, were built by Emergency One on the upgraded Scania P280 chassis. Also in 2013 a Special Incident Support Unit (Heavy Rescue Tender) was built by W. H. Bence on a Scania 6x2 chassis and fitted with a Hiab crane. Two more Compact Water Tenders were built on the MAN TGL 12.240 chassis in 2013 but this time by Emergency One. The latest pumping appliances are five MAN TGL 12.250 Water Tenders built by Emergency One and delivered in 2015.

2013 Scania 6x2 Special Incident Support Unit reg. no. WX13 AYG built by W. H. Bence (photo – The Author)

MAN TGL 12.250 Water Tender Ladder reg. no. WU15 HNJ built by Emergency One, one of five delivered in 2015 (photo – Andy Spence)

Gloucestershire Fire and Rescue Service currently has two wholetime, three wholetime/retained, one day-crewed/retained and sixteen retained fire stations. The operational fleet includes thirty-three pumping appliances, three Small Fire Units, two Aerial Ladder Platforms, one Foam and Water Carrier, one Heavy Rescue Tender, one Incident Command Unit, one Environmental Protection Unit, one Damage Control Unit, one Breathing Apparatus Support Unit, one Incident Support Unit, twelve Light 4x4Vehicles, two Incident Response Units, three Prime Movers, one Haz-Mat pod, one High Volume Pumping Unit pod, one High Volume Hose Laying Unit pod and one Mass Decontamination Dis-robe pod. There are also a number of trailer units including two Cliff Rescue Units, two Inshore Rescue Boats, one Canteen Unit and one Welfare Unit.

CHAPTER 6
ISLES OF SCILLY

Prior to the early 1940's, fires in St. Mary's were dealt with by employees of The Duchy of Cornwall. Following the outbreak of the Second World War, a volunteer fire service was formed on St. Mary's comprised of a Dennis Trailer Pump towed by a "cut-down" Ford car, the prime use of which at the time was cutting the grass on the golf links!

Isles of Scilly Fire Brigade 1948- 1997
Appliances known to have served on the Isles of Scilly

Built	Type	Chassis	Body	Reg. No.
	ATV	Austin K2		
1950	Water Tender (1)	Austin Loadstar	Home Office	NAF 10
	L4P (1)	Austin Gipsy		854 DRL
1956	Water Tender (1)	Bedford SH	Miles	TFJ 666
	Tractor (2)	Fordson Dexta		
1966	L4P	Austin Gipsy		SCY 203L
1969	Water Tender (3)	Bedford TK	Carmichael	RTF 815G
	Tractor (2)	Massey Ferguson MF135		
1974	Water Tender (1)	Bedford TKEL	HCB-Angus	OOU 449M
1976	L4P (1)	Land Rover Series III	Carmichael	MCV 569P
1979	L4P (1)	Land Rover Series III	Carmichael	YGL 138T
1981	L4P (1)	Land Rover Series III/	Cornwall FB	ECV 854V
	Tractor (4)	Zetor 5211		Q494 XAF
1984	L4P (1)	Land Rover Series III	Cornwall FB	B569 BAF
1986	Tractor (4)	Zetor 5211		D611 KRL
1990	Compact Water Tender (1)	Renault Dodge S507S	Cornwall FB	H625 FGL
1991	Tractor (4)	Zetor 5211		J647 ODV
1997	Water Tender	Mercedes-Benz 1124AF	Carmichael	P156 SCY
2010	Brigade Response Vehicle	Toyota HiLux	Cornwall FB	WK10 AFZ

(1)   Ex-Cornwall Fire Brigade
(2)   Towed a trailer pump
(3)   Ex-Lancashire Fire Service
(4)   Tows an Equipment Trailer

In 1948 the Isles of Scilly became a Fire Authority and took over the volunteer fire brigade which, by this time, was equipped with two Beresford Trailer Pumps towed by an Austin Towing Vehicle (ATV). The Brigade was housed in the Fire Station at Bona Vista until 1953 when the unit was moved to a building at Porthcressa, which in 1984 was replaced by the current fire station at Porthmellon.

The ATV was in use until 1969 when a 1950 Austin Loadstar Water Tender was purchased from Cornwall Fire Brigade. Cornwall continued to supply redundant appliances to the islands with a 1956 Bedford SH Water Tender built by Alfred Miles and an Austin Gipsy L4P. A new Austin Gipsy L4P was delivered to the islands in 1966 but was not registered until 1974 due to the fact that at the time the islands' vehicles were not liable to carry registration plates. A 1969 Bedford TK Water Tender built by Carmichaels was obtained second-hand from Lancashire Fire Service and arrived on the islands during the 1980s. Two redundant Land Rover Series III L4Ps were later delivered from Cornwall Fire Brigade; a 1976 Carmichael version arrived in 1989 with a 1981 version built in Cornwall's workshops arriving in 1995. Yet another ex-Cornwall appliance to arrive was a 1974 Bedford TK Water Tender built by HCB-Angus.

This 1950 Austin Loadstar Water Tender arrived in 1969
(The Gary Chapman Collection)

1956 Bedford SH Water Tender with Miles bodywork reg. no. TFJ 666
(The Gary Chapman Collection)

This Austin Gipsy L4P reg. no. SCY 203L was delivered in 1966
(The Gary Chapman Collection)

1969 Bedford TK Water Tender reg. no. RTF 815G built by Carmichaels which originally served as a Water Tender Escape with Lancashire County Fire Service (The Gary Chapman Collection)

This 1974 Bedford TKEL Water Tender reg. no. OOU 449M originally served in Cornwall (The Gary Chapman Collection)

This 1981 Land Rover L4P reg. no. ECV 854V arrived on the islands in 1995 (The Gary Chapman Collection)

A 1999 arrival was this 1979 Land Rover L4P reg. no. YGL 138T built by Carmichaels, seen here towing an equipment trailer (The Gary Chapman Collection)

Bryher's Zetor Tractor seen here towing an early version of an Equipment Trailer (The Gary Chapman Collection)

Another Equipment Trailer was this one which was based at St. Agnes and shows the BA stowage (The Gary Chapman Collection)

Isles of Scilly Fire and Rescue Service 1997 – onwards

In 1997 the brigade was renamed the Isles of Scilly Fire and Rescue Service and the same year a new Water Tender was purchased, built by Carmichaels, on a Mercedes-Benz 1124AF chassis followed in 1999 by an ex-Cornwall Fire Brigade 1979 Land Rover L4P. Another ex-Cornwall appliance arrived in 2006 after serving at Polruan Fire Station. This was a 1990 Renault Dodge S507S Compact Water Tender. The latest appliance to arrive was delivered in 2010, a Toyota

HiLux 4x4 Light Vehicle which was fitted out by Cornwall's workshops before delivery. This was converted in 2014 to a Brigade Response Vehicle, by Evems Ltd of Doncaster, to give the service a better off-road capability and access to areas of limited access.

Today the Isles of Scilly Fire and Rescue Service is the smallest in the United Kingdom and is a fully retained service. There are fire stations on five of the islands; St. Mary's, Bryher, St. Agnes, St. Martin's and Tresco. In addition the airport has its own fire and rescue service. All the stations are multi-agency with the outer island stations housing the ambulance service co-responders and HM Coastguard auxiliaries and their equipment. On St. Mary's the station only houses the fire and ambulance services with the Coastguards having their own separate facilities. The Fire and Rescue Service work in close co-operation with Cornwall Fire and Rescue Service sharing a Chief Fire Officer and emergency calls are routed to Cornwall's Control Room who operate the turn-out systems for the Islands' crews. For any incidents on the outer islands St Mary's are mobilised as well as the local station. The St Mary's crew proceed to the quay and whilst en-route contact the local island to get information on the incident and if necessary a crew and the necessary equipment is taken to the incident on the ambulance response boat.

The current fleet consists of two Water Tenders, one Brigade Response Vehicle, three Tractors and three Equipment Trailers. In recent years the Equipment Trailers have been redesigned and rebuilt by a local engineer and all carry 900 litres (200 gallons) of water, a portable pump, breathing apparatus, ladders, a lighting mast and a generator. It should be noted that each station has a number of volunteer firefighters attached to it who cover for crewing shortages e.g. holidays, sickness etc.

St. Mary's

St. Mary's being the largest island and with most risk is manned by a Station Manager, two Watch Managers, two Crew Managers and twelve firefighters plus four volunteers operating a Mercedes-Benz Water Tender and a Toyota Brigade Response Vehicle. St. Mary's appliances also carry the specialist equipment for chemical incidents and road traffic incidents. Nine of the firefighters are also employed at St. Mary's Airport and are CAA licensed firefighters and there is close co-operation between the two services.

St Mary's 1997 Mercedes-Benz 1124AF Water Tender reg. no.
P156 SCY built by Carmichaels (The Gary Chapman Collection)

Delivered in 2010 Toyota Hilux reg. no. WA10 AFZ was built as a
Light Towing Vehicle (The Gary Chapman Collection)

The same vehicle after conversion in 2014 into a Brigade
Response Vehicle (photo – Kevin James)

Bryher
Bryher Fire Station has a complement of one Watch Manager, one Crew Manager, six firefighters
and two volunteers who operate with a Zetor Tractor and an Equipment Trailer.

St. Agnes
St. Agnes Fire Station is also staffed by one Watch Manager, one Crew Manager, six firefighters
plus two volunteers and again operates a Zetor Tractor and an Equipment Trailer.

St. Martin's
Also equipped with a Zetor Tractor and Equipment Trailer, St. Martin's Fire Station is staffed by
one Watch Manager, one Crew Manager, six firefighters and one volunteer.

One of the modern Equipment Trailers is this one based at St. Martins
(unknown photographer)

Tresco's appliance is this1991 Dodge S75 Midi Water Tender reg. no.
H625 FGL which was originally in service with Cornwall Fire Brigade
(photo – Gary Chapman)

Tresco

Tresco Fire Station has one Watch Manager, one Crew Manager, six firefighters with two
volunteers and they crew a Renault Dodge S507S Compact Water Tender which was refurbished
in 2014. The station has a limited capacity to deal with vehicle rescues by carrying some crash
rescue equipment.

Tresco Heliport 1983 - 2012

From 1983 to 2012 there was a heliport on Tresco which had a fire crew operated by Tresco
Estate workers which was separate from the local authority fire crew.

Appliances known to have served at Tresco Heliport

Built	Type	Chassis	Body	Reg. No.
	L4P	Land Rover 109	Carmichael	954 EAE
1984	Rapid Intervention Vehicle	Reynolds Boughton RB44	HCB-Angus	B551 RLO
1985	Rapid Intervention Vehicle	Reynolds Boughton RB44	HCB-Angus	C874 KRO

In use at Tresco Heliport was this Land Rover reg. no. 954 EAE, note the additional trolley extinguishers mounted on the front
(The Gary Chapman Collection)

This 1984 Reynolds Boughton RB44 reg. no. B551 RLO operated at Tresco Heliport as a Rapid Intervention Vehicle (The Gary Chapman Collection)

St. Mary's Airport 1964 – onwards

The airport first opened in August 1939 and is the only airport serving the Isles of Scilly. In 1964 a helicopter service was started linking St. Marys with Penzance Heliport on the mainland followed in 1972 with a fixed wing service from Lands End Airport (St Just). After being in operation for forty-eight years, the helicopter service ceased flying in 2012. Currently there is only one airline operating at St Mary's Airport with flights to and from Lands End, Newquay and Exeter airports.

The Airport Fire and Rescue Service is a separate entity to the local authority service although nine of the airport's crew are also retained crew members at St Mary's Fire Station and the two services work in close co-operation with each other. Currently there are two Foam Tenders on the run at the airport although normally only one is crewed plus a Toyota Hilux which tows a water trailer.

Appliances known to have served at St Mary's Airport

Built	Type	Chassis	Body	Reg. No.
	Pump (1)	Bedford RLHZ		RXP 708
	Water/Foam Carrier	Bedford RLHC		HUC 512
1977	Rapid Intervention Vehicle	Dodge Power Ram		JHO 551S
1983	L4V (2)	Land Rover Series III		FCK 901Y
1985	L4P	Land Rover Series III	Cornwall FB	B569 BAF
	Foam Tender (3)	Scammell Nubian Mk 10	Carmichael	G24 SCY
1995	Foam Tender	Mercedes-Benz 1124AF	Carmichael	M132 SCY
2006	L4V (4)	Toyota HiLux		WK56 AOY

(1)   Ex-AFS pump repainted red
(2)   Towed a Perren Trailer
(3)   Ex-RAF
(4)   Tows a water trailer

Two Bedford appliances seen here at St. Mary's Airport (*l to r*) Bedford RLHC Water/Foam Carrier and ex-AFS Bedford RLHZ Pump (The Gary Chapman Collection)

1977 Dodge Power Ram Rapid Intervention Vehicle reg. no.
JHO 551S and Land Rover L4V reg. no. FCK 901Y
(The Gary Chapman Collection)

One of St. Mary's Airport front-line Foam Tenders is this 1995
Mercedes-Benz 1124AF reg. no. M132 SCY built by
Carmichaels (The Gary Chapman Collection)

This Scammell Nubian Foam Tender reg. no. G24 SCY built by
Carmichaels is also on the run at St. Mary's Airport
(The Gary Chapman Collection)

The 2006 Toyota Hilux Light Vehicle reg. no. WK56 AOY which tows a water trailer (photo – Peter Adams)

CHAPTER 7
WILTSHIRE

Wiltshire Fire Brigade was one of 141 brigades formed on 1st April 1948 on the de-nationalisation of the National Fire Service., with some villages losing their units and having fire cover provided by other stations within the new brigade. Wiltshire covers a large area, with its towns, villages and the city of Salisbury located around the periphery of Salisbury Plain. The brigade's area has remained unchanged since its inception in 1948 despite the many changes to local government which have affected most of the brigades in the UK.

Wiltshire Fire Brigade 1948-2006

The brigade initially comprised of 24 fire stations which included Aldbourne, Box, Market Lavington and Ramsbury which were known as Local Light Units. Box was closed almost immediately while Market Lavington was closed in 1953 and the volunteer station at Aldbourne closed in the mid 1960s.

Fire Appliances known to have been taken over by Wiltshire Fire Brigade in 1948

Built	Type	Chassis	Body	Reg. No.
1927	Pump Escape	Dennis		MW 2217
1927	Pump Escape	Dennis		MW 6125
1928	Pump	Dennis		
1931	Pump	Dennis		WV 1627
1932	Pump	Dennis		MR9887
1933	Pump	Morris Commercial		WV 4286
1933	Pump Escape	Dennis		WV 3993
1935	Towing Vehicle	Fordson		WV 7991
1936	Pump Escape	Leyland FK6		AAM 695
1938	Towing Vehicle	Dennis		WV 9807
1938	Towing Vehicle	Morris Commercial		AMR 573
1939	Hosereel Tender	Dennis Ace	New World	CAM 710
1939	Hosereel Tender	Dennis Ace	New World	CAM 711
1939	Pump	Dennis Light 4	New World	CHR 147
1939	Emergency Tender	Morris		CHR 514
1939	Pump Escape	Leyland FKT2		CHR 598
1940	Towing Vehicle	Bedford		CHR 826
1940	Towing Vehicle	Fordson		CHR 968
1940	Towing Vehicle	Fordson		CHR 969
1940	Towing Vehicle	Fordson		CMW 109
1940	Pump Escape	Leyland FK8A		CMW 356

Built	Type	Chassis	Body	Reg. No.
1942	ATV	Austin K2		GGN 664
1942	Hose Layer	Fordson 7v		GGN 701
1942	WrT A (1)	Fordson 7v		GGU 919
1942	ATV	Austin K2		GGX 419
1942	Turntable Ladder	Leyland TLM	Merryweather 100ft	GHW 415
1942	Salvage Tender (2)	Austin K2		GLE 587
1942	WrT A (1)	Austin K4		GLM 940
1942	ATV	Austin K2		GLR 537
1942	ATV	Austin K2		GLR 924
1942	ATV	Austin K2		GLR 937
1942	ATV	Austin K2		GLT 81
1942	ATV	Austin K2		GLT 118
1942	ATV	Austin K2		GLT 320
1942	ATV	Austin K2		GLT 321
1942	ATV	Austin K2		GLT 859
1942	WrT A (1)	Fordson 7v		GLW 214
1942	WrT A (1)	Fordson		GLW 362
1943	Pump Escape (3)	Austin K4		GLY 219
1943	Pump Escape (3)	Austin K4		GLY 935
1943	Turntable Ladder	Leyland Beaver	Merryweather 100ft	GXA 61
1943	Pump Escape (3)	Austin K4		GXA 73
1943	ATV	Austin K2		GXH 72
1943	ATV	Austin K2		GXH 74
1943	Hosereel Tender (2)	Austin K2		GXH 166
1943	Hosereel Tender (2)	Austin K2		GXH 371
1943	Hosereel Tender (2)	Austin K2		GXH 372
1943	ATV	Austin K2		GXH 386
1943	ATV	Austin K2		GXH 523
1943	ATV	Austin K2		GXH 671
1943	ATV	Austin K2		GXH 683
1943	Hosereel Tender (2)	Austin K2		GXH 684
1944	WrT A (1)	Austin K4		GXM 112
1944	WrT A (1)	Fordson 7v		GXM 249
1944	WrT A (1)	Fordson 7v		GXM 260
1944	WrT A (1)	Fordson 7v		GXM 299
1944	WrT A (1)	Dodge		GXM 567
1944	Turntable Ladder	Austin K4	Merryweather 60ft	GXN 217
1944	Hose Layer	Fordson 7v		GXN 979
1944	WrT A (1)	Dodge		GXO 513
1944	WrT A (1)	Dodge		GXO 544
1946	WrT A (4)	Bedford QL		GYR 811

(1)   Ex Major Dam Unit
(2)   Ex ATV
(3)   Ex Escape Carrying Unit
(4)   Ex Ministry of Defence

It was not until 1952 that the first post-war appliances arrived with a delivery of four Commer QX Water Tenders built by James Whitson followed by a further seventeen Water Tenders and four Water Tender Escapes built on the Commer QX chassis which were purchased between 1953 and 1960 but now built by Alfred Miles of Cheltenham. Two Dennis appliances had been delivered in 1954; a F12 Pump Escape and a F8 Water Tender. Also in 1954 a Leyland Comet Pump was purchased built by Windovers. In 1958 Wiltshire's workshops converted an Austin A503 workshops vehicle into an Emergency Tender. The first Bedford appliance to appear in the post-war fleet was a Miles built Water Tender based on the J4 chassis. In 1962 a new Turntable Ladder was delivered by David Haydon built on a Bedford SL chassis and fitted with Magirus 100 feet ladders. With the introduction of the Bedford TK chassis Wiltshire entered into a contract with Hampshire Car Bodies, later to become HCB-Angus (HCB-A), and eleven Water Tenders were delivered between 1962 and 1968. During the same period two Control Units were supplied; one built by Mumfords in 1964 and the other by HCB-A in 1966. A Bedford TK based Foam Tender/Hose Layer was also delivered in 1966 built by Lee Motors. During the 1960s twelve Land Rover light vehicles had been purchased, five of which were converted to Rescue Tenders. Following the disbandment of the Auxiliary Fire Service (AFS) in 1968 Wiltshire obtained a Recovery Vehicle built on a Bedford RLHZ chassis. Another new Turntable Ladder

1960 Commer QX Water Tender reg. no. UWV 569 built by Alfred Miles (photo – The Author's Collection)

1962 Bedford SL Turntable Ladders reg. no. WWV 439 built by David Haydon and fitted with Magirus ladders (photo – Mike Lawmon)

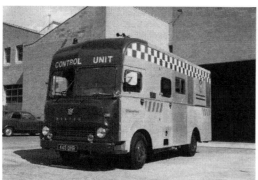
1964 Bedford TK Control Unit reg. no. 445 DHR
built by Mumfords (photo – Mike Lawmon)

Bedford TK Water Tender reg. no. BHR 369B one of
two delivered in 1964 by HCB (photo – Mike Lawmon)

1967 Land Rover 109 reg. no. JHR 486E one of
five converted to Rescue Tenders in 1969
(photo – Mike Lawmon)

1969 AEC Mercury Turntable Ladder reg. no. MMR
217G built by Merryweathers
(photo – Mike Lawmon)

was purchased in 1969 built on the AEC Mercury chassis with Merryweather 100 feet ladders

Between 1970 and 1972 HCB-A delivered eleven Water Tenders built on the Bedford TKEL chassis. In 1973 a decision was made to change the chassis supplier to Dodge and by 1976 eleven Water Tenders had been delivered; five built by HCB-A and six by Carmichaels all built on the K850 chassis. Meanwhile in 1974 Merryweathers had built a Pump Hydraulic Platform fitted with Simon SS50 booms. Merryweathers also built two Emergency/Salvage Tenders on the Dodge K850 chassis which were delivered in 1974 and 1975. These were later converted to a Damage Control Unit and an Incident Support Unit. 1976 saw a Range Rover Commando Rescue Tender enter the fleet built by Carmichaels. With the introduction of the upgraded Dodge K1113 chassis ten Water Tenders were purchased between 1977 and 1979; three built by ERF with Firefighter bodywork, three by Angloco and four by Cheshire Fire Engineering (CFE). The last appliance purchased in the 1970s was a Turntable Ladder built on the Dodge G1690 chassis by Carmichaels fitted with Magirus 100 feet ladders and delivered in 1979. The use of Land Rovers as light vehicles continued and by 1995 a further seventeen had been purchased.

HCB-A continued to supply Water Tenders now built on the Dodge G1313 chassis and between 1980 and 1982 had delivered six whilst CFE had delivered three in 1981. Also in 1981 Carmichaels had built a Rescue Tender on a Dodge S66 chassis whilst Bensons had supplied a Control Unit/Canteen Van in 1982 built on a Dodge G09 chassis. In 1983 there was a delivery of three Water Tenders built on the Dennis SS131 chassis. There was a return to the Dodge G13 chassis in 1985 and twelve more Water Tenders were delivered by 1988; ten by HCB-A between 1985 and 1987 followed in 1988 by two built by Mountain Range. 1988 also saw the

1974 Dodge K1050 Pump Hydraulic Platform reg. no. PMR 714M built by Merryweathers with Simon SS50 booms (The Roy Yeoman Collection)

1975 Dodge K850 Damage Control Unit reg. no. GHR 618N built by Merryweather (photo – Colin Dunford)

1976 Range Rover Commando 6x4 Rescue Tender reg. no. KMR 673P built by Carmichael (photo – Mike Lawmon)

1976 Dodge K850 Water Tender Ladder reg. no. KMW 891P built by Carmichaels (photo – Colin Dunford)

1979 Dodge G1690 Turntable Ladder reg. no. XMW 758T built by Carmichael with Magirus 100 feet ladders (photo – Mike Lawmon)

1981 Leyland Clydesdale Water Carrier reg. no. XYA 369W built by Wincanton (photo – Colin Dunford)

1982 Dodge G09 Control Unit/Canteen Van reg. no. NAM 362X
built by Benson (photo – Colin Dunford)

1983 Dennis SS131 Water Tender Ladder reg. no.
RMW 22Y (photo – Colin Dunford)

1984 Dennis DF1616 Prime Mover reg. no. A955
XOB and HazMat pod (photo – Colin Dunford)

1988 Dodge G13 Water Tender Ladder reg. no.
E554 XMR built by Mountain Range
(photo – Colin Dunford)

1988 Dodge G16 Prime Mover reg. no. E555 XMR
loaded with the Foam Unit Pod
(photo – Mike Lawmon)

introduction of a pod system when a Bulk Foam Unit pod and an Incident Command Unit pod were delivered. To carry them a Dodge G16 Prime Mover was purchased with Multilift fitments. Three Leyland Clydesdale Milk Tankers were purchased between 1989 and 1991 and converted to Water Carriers.

The first Mercedes-Benz appliance appeared in the fleet in 1990 with the delivery of an Aerial Ladder Platform built by Angloco on the Mercedes-Benz 2228 chassis and fitted with Bronto Skylift 28-2TI booms. Also in 1990 Mountain Range built five Compact Pumps and three Rescue Tenders all on the Mercedes-Benz LN1120AF chassis. In 1991 just one Water Tender was purchased; a Dennis SS237 again built by Mountain Range. Between 1992 and 1993 seven Water Tenders were built by Reliance Mercury now on the Mercedes-Benz LN1124 chassis. Other appliances delivered in 1993 were a Pump Hydraulic Platform built by Saxon on a Scania 93M-280 chassis with Italmec 29M booms and a Rescue Tender built by Devcoplan on a Mercedes-Benz LN1124AF chassis. The Mercedes-Benz LN1124 chassis continued to be used and between 1994 and 1995 six more Water Tenders were delivered; five built by Emergency One and one by Carmichaels. In 1995 Wiltshire purchased a 1984 Dennis DF1616 Prime Mover and HazMat pod from West Midlands Fire Service. 1995 also saw the start of a contract with John Dennis Coachbuilders (JDC) for the supply of Water Tenders and by 2007 twenty-nine had been

1990 Mercedes-Benz 2228 Aerial Ladder Platform reg. no. G459 NMW built by Angloco and fitted with Bronto Skylift 28 metre booms
(photo – Colin Dunford)

1990 Mercedes-Benz LN1120AF Compact Pump reg. no. G465 NMW built by Mountain Range
(photo – Mike Lawmon)

1990 Mercedes-Benz LN920AF Rescue Tender reg. no. G470 NMW built by Mountain Range (photo – Colin Dunford)

delivered on the Dennis Sabre chassis. A new Prime Mover was bought in 1995 built on an ERF ES8 chassis and in 1996 another Pump Hydraulic Platform was built this time by GB Fire on an ERF EC10 6x4 chassis fitted with Interlift 25.5 metre booms. Another Prime Mover was built in 1998 on a Iveco-Ford Eurocargo chassis and between 1999 and 2001 three Water Carriers were built by Wincanton on the Iveco-Ford Eurocargo chassis.

The new millennium had seen a change in the supplier of light vehicles with the delivery of a Mazda 4x4 Truckman in 2000 followed by four more by 2004. In 2002 four Emergency Support Units (Rescue Tenders) were built by JDC on the Mercedes-Benz Econic 1824 chassis followed in 2003 and 2004 by two Aerial Ladder Platforms built on the same chassis by Angloco fitted with Bronto F32RL booms.

1992 Mercedes-Benz LN1124 Water Tender Ladder reg. no. J288 HMR built by Reliance Mercury (photo – Colin Dunford)

1993 Scania P93M-280 6x4 Pump Hydraulic Platform reg. no. K629 OAM built by Saxon with Italmec 29 metre booms (photo – Mike Lawmon)

1995 ERF ES8 Prime Mover reg. no. N170 KAM fitted with Multilift equipment. Seen here loaded with the Damage Control Unit pod
(Unknown photographer)

1996 ERF EC10 6x4 Pump Hydraulic Platform reg. no. P532 SMW built by GB Fire and fitted with Interlift 25.5 metre booms (photo – Mike Lawmon)

2001 Iveco Eurocargo 180E23 Water Carrier reg. no. Y523 UMW built by Wincanton (photo – Mike Lawmon)

Mercedes-Benx Econic Emergency Support Unit reg. no. WU02 KLJ built JDC, one of four delivered in 2002 (photo – Mike Lawmon)

2004 Dennis Sabre Water Tender Ladder reg. no. WX04 WVB with JDC bodywork (photo – Mike Lawmon)

2004 Mercedes-Benz Econic Aerial Ladder Platform reg. no. WU54 EKA built by Angloco and fitted with Bronto F32RL booms (photo – Malcolm Thompson)

Wiltshire Fire & Rescue Service 2006 - onwards

In 2006 the brigade changed its title to Wiltshire Fire and Rescue to reflect the broader role which it carried out. Also that year there was another change in the supplier of light vehicles when a Ford Ranger 4x4 Light Pump was delivered followed in 2008 by two Water Rescue Units all built by JDC. In 2008 three Water Tenders were delivered built by JDC on the Scania P270-CP31 chassis followed by a further three in 2009. Also in 2009 an Incident Command Unit was built by W. H. Bence on an Iveco Daily chassis and fitted with Excelerate satellite communications equipment.

Two Rescue Units, combining the roles of Water Rescue and Animal Rescue, were delivered in 2010 built on the Mercedes-Benz Sprinter chassis to replace the Ford Rangers which proved too small to carry the required equipment. The upgraded Scania P280-CP31 was introduced in 2010 and by 2013 nine Water Tenders had been delivered by JDC on this chassis. Meanwhile in 2012 two Operational Support Units had been built by Essex Bodies on the Scania P320 6x2 chassis carrying Paflinger/Cryler Forklift Trucks. A new concept was delivered in 2014 with the introduction of a Heavy Rescue Unit built by JDC on a Mercedes-Benz Atego chassis to replace the four Emergency Support Units.

2008 Ford Ranger Water Rescue Unit reg. no. WX58 LUY built by JDC (photo – Malcolm Thompson)

2009 Iveco Daily Incident Command Unit reg. no. WX59 GWG built by W. H. Bence (photo – Malcolm Thompson)

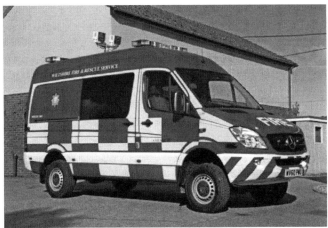

2010 Mercedes-Benz 4x4 Rescue Unit reg. no. WV60 PWU
built by Rygor to carry out the roles of both Water Rescue and
Animal Rescue (photo – Malcolm Thompson)

2012 Scania P280 Water Tender Ladder reg. no. WX62 AVU
built by JDC (photo – Malcolm Thompson)

2012 Scania P320 Operational Support Unit reg no. WX12 ETR
built by Essex Bodies and carrying a Paflinger/Crayler Forklift
Truck (photo – Malcolm Thompson)

2014 Heavy Rescue Tender reg. no. WX64 HEV built by JDC on
a Mercedes-Benz Atego chassis (photo – Malcolm Thompson)

The service now has two wholetime/retained, one day-crewed, three day-crewed/retained and eighteen retained fire stations. The fleet consists of thirty-four pumping appliances, two aerial appliances, one Heavy Rescue Unit, four Water Carriers, two Land Rover Pumps, two Incident Command Units, two Operational Support Units, two Animal/Water Rescue Units, two Rope Rescue Units, one Incident Response Unit, two Prime Movers, one Mass Decontamination Dis-robe pod and one Mass Decontamination Re-robe pod.

In November 2014 an agreement was made with Dorset Fire and Rescue Service to amalgamate the two authorities into one large service on the 1st April 2016. To be known as the Dorset and Wiltshire Fire and Rescue Service the first move was the opening of a Combined Command and Control Room at Wiltshire's Potterne headquarters in August 2015. The headquarters of the new combined service will be in Salisbury.

CHAPTER 8
THE FIRE SERVICE COLLEGE

The first central training centre set up in the UK was at Saltdean near Brighton which opened in1941 to train staff officers for the National Fire Service. After World War II the college at Saltdean closed and in 1949 the Home Office opened the Senior Staff College at Wotton House, Dorking in Surrey, to train senior officers from all over the country. In June 1966, they decided to do the same for the lower ranks and established a Fire Service College. The College was built on a disused RAF wartime airfield just outside Moreton in Marsh, a village in Gloucestershire. The airfield had remained operational until the late 1950s and the government then used the base to teach emergency fire fighting to military personnel undergoing their National Service.

The Home Office opened the College on the 500 acre site in 1968. The Staff College at Dorking was closed in 1981 and all training was then transferred to Moreton in Marsh.

The initial appliance fleet consisted of a 1951 Dennis F12 Pump Escape, six Auxiliary Fire Service Bedford RLHZ 4x4 Emergency Pumps (Green Goddesses) and an AFS Thorneycroft Breakdown Lorry. Three new appliances were delivered in 1968 built on the AEC Mercury chassis; two Turntable Ladders with Merryweather 100 feet ladders and a Dual Purpose appliance again built by Merryweather. There was a large influx of new appliances in 1969 with Dennis Brothers supplying one F36 Water Tender, one F43 Pump Escape, one F108 Water Tender and one F121 Hydraulic Platform fitted with Simon SS70 booms. The same year four Bedford TK Water Tenders were built by Carmichaels and a Foam Tender was built by Pyrene again on the Bedford TK chassis.

1968 AEC Mercury 7 Turntable Ladder reg. no. ULR 67F fitted with
Merryweather 100 feet ladders (photo – Bob Smith)

1968 AEC Mercury 7 Dual Purpose Appliance reg. no. ULR
69F built by Merryweather (photo – Bob Smith)

1969 Dennis F43 Pump Escape reg. no. VLU 202G
(The Author's Collection)

1969 Bedford TK Water Tender reg. no. VLU 205G built by
Carmichaels with a 'Vista View' cab (The Author's Collection)

1969 Dennis F121 Hydraulic Platform reg. no. VLU 214G fitted with Simon SS70 booms (photo - Bob Smith)

1970 Bedford TK Control Unit reg. no. ALT 467H built by Plaxtons (photo - Bob Smith)

This Bedford TK Pump Escape reg. no. ALT 468H built by HCB-Angus was delivered in 1970 (photo – Bob Smith)

In 1970 a pair of Pump Escapes was built by HCB-Angus (HCB-A) on the Bedford TK chassis and Plaxtons built a Control Unit, a Hose Layer and a Salvage Tender all on the Bedford TK chassis. The same year Dennis Brothers delivered a F108 Emergency Tender. The next appliances arrived in 1975 and consisted of four Water Tenders; one built by HCB-Angus on the Dodge K850 chassis, a Dennis D type, a Ford D1014 built by Carmichaels and an ERF 84PF built with ERF Firefighter bodywork. In 1977 HCB-A delivered a Bedford TK Water Tender with a Crew Safety Vehicle body. An unusual Water Tender was also purchased in 1977 built by Chubb on a Reynolds Boughton chassis. Known as the Pacesetter it had a front mounted pump and low level lockers and folding entrance doors for easy access for the crew. The last appliances purchased in the 1970s were two 1978 Dodge K1113 Water Tenders built by HCB-A.

1980 saw the introduction of the Dennis RS chassis into the fleet when Dennis Brothers delivered a trio of RS133 Water Tender Ladders. Other appliances delivered that year were a Dodge G1613 Foam Tender and Range Rover Commando Rescue Tender both built by Carmichaels. In 1981 Carmichaels supplied a pair of Bedford TKG Water Tender Ladders. The only delivery in 1983 was a Hydraulic Platform built by Angloco on a Shelvoke & Drewry WY chassis and fitted with Simon SS220 booms. Saxons delivered three Bedford TKG Water Tenders in 1984 and the same year Carmichaels built a Turntable Ladder on a Shelvoke & Drewry chassis fitted with Magirus ladders. With the demise of the London Salvage Corps in 1984 the College obtained from them a Dodge G1313 Damage Control Unit built by HCB-A. In 1985 three 'specials' were delivered all on the Bedford TK chassis; a Breathing Apparatus Tender built by Saxons, a Chemical Incident Unit with Victory bodywork and a Control Unit built by Angloco.

1970 Dennis F108 Emergency Tender reg. no. ALT 470H (The Author's Collection)

1975 Dodge K850 Water Tender Ladder reg. no. GJD 805N built by HCB-Angus (The Author's Collection)

1975 Dennis D Water Tender reg. no. GJD 806N (The Author's Collection)

1975 Ford D1014 Water Tender Ladder reg. no. GJD 807N built by Carmichaels (The Author's Collection)

1975 ERF 84PF Water Tender Ladder reg. no. KUC 701P built with ERF Firefighter bodywork (The Author's Collection)

1977 Bedford TK Water Tender Ladder reg. no. OYH 414R built by HCB-Angus with Crew Safety Vehicle bodywork (The Author's Collection)

The distinctive Chubb Pacesetter Water Tender Ladder reg. no. OYH 417R was delivered in 1977. (photo – Bob Smith)

Dennis RS133 Water Tender Ladder reg. no. CYH 440V was one of three delivered in 1980 (photo – Colin Dunford)

Carmichaels built this Dodge G1613 Foam Tender reg. no. CYH 441V in 1980 (photo – Bob Smith)

1980 Range Rover Commando 6x4 Rescue Tender reg. no. CYH 442V built by Carmichaels (The Author's Collection)

1981 Shelvoke & Drewry WY Hydraulic Platform reg. no. KYY 295X was built by Angloco with Simon booms (The Author's Collection)

Bedford TKG Water Tender Ladder reg. no. GUL 273W was one of a pair delivered by Carmichaels in 1981 (photo – Colin Dunford)

This Shelvoke & Drewry Turntable Ladder reg. no. NYL 712Y was delivered in 1984 by Carmichaels fitted with Magirus DL30E ladders (photo – Bob Smith)

Bedford TKG Water Tender Ladder reg. no. NYL 737Y built by Saxons was one of three delivered in 1984 (photo – Colin Dunford)

This Dodge G1313 Salvage Tender reg. no. ALY 911Y was obtained by the College following the disbandment of the London Salvage Corps in 1984 (photo – Colin Dunford)

This Bedford TK Chemical Incident Unit reg. no. B839 WYM built by Victory was delivered in 1985 (photo – Colin Dunford)

Between 1986 and 1987 Carmichaels delivered three Water Tender Ladders built on the Dodge G13 chassis. A new Hydraulic Platform was built in 1988 by Saxons on a Dodge G16L chassis fitted with Simon SS220 booms. In 1989 four Water Tenders were purchased; two built on the Leyland Freighter 16-17 chassis; one by Carmichaels and one by Fulton & Wylie and the other two built by Saxons on the Volvo FL6.14 chassis.

Saxons supplied another pair of Volvo FL6.14 Water Tenders in 1990. Also the same year John Dennis Coachbuilders (JDC) delivered a Dennis Rapier Water Tender followed by a similar appliance in 1992. Meanwhile in 1991 Carmichaels had delivered a pair of Water Tenders built on the Mercedes Benz 1120 chassis. A 1989 built Leyland Freighter Prime Mover had been purchased from the Royal Aircraft Establishment at Farnborough in the mid 1990s along with a Control Unit pod. With the College commencing airfield firefighting training two Rapid Intervention Vehicles and one Crash Tender all built on the Gloster Saro Protector chassis were purchased in 1994. In 1996 a replacement Prime Mover based on the Renault Midliner M200 chassis and fitted with Multilift equipment was purchased. 1997 saw three new Water Tenders supplied purchased; one on the Dennis Sabre chassis and two built on the Volvo FL6.14 chassis all by Carmichaels. Five second-hand Water Tenders were also purchased in 1997; four Dennis RS135s Water Tenders originally in service with Norfolk Fire Service and one Dodge G13 built for Gloucestershire Fire and Rescue Service all of 1984 vintage.

Dodge G13 Water Tender Ladder reg. no. D735 FHM which was built by Carmichaels in 1987 (photo – Colin Dunford)

1988 Dodge G16L Hydraulic Platform reg. no. E420 MYH built by Saxons and fitted with Simon SS220 booms. (photo – Colin Dunford)

Leyland Freighter 16-17 Water Tender Ladder reg. no. F416 NYY, one of a pair built by Carmichaels in 1989 (photo – Colin Dunford)

1989 Leyland Freighter Prime Mover reg. no. F424 PPG loaded with a Control Unit pod built by Ray Smiths (photo – Colin Dunford)

JDC built this 1990 Dennis Rapier Water Tender Ladder reg. no. G117 WPK (photo – Colin Dunford)

1991 Mercedes-Benz 1120AF Water Tender Ladder reg. no. H455 XHX built by Carmichaels (photo – Colin Dunford)

This Dennis Sabre Water Tender Ladder was built by Carmichaels in 1997 (photo – The Author)

This 1997 Volvo FL6.14 Water Tender Ladder reg. no. R497 YRP was built by Excalibur (photo – The Author)

This unusual looking demonstrator Spartan Water Tender Ladder was built by Emergency One in 1997 (photo – Colin Dunford)

An unusual Water Tender arrived at the College in 1997 when Emergency One loaned a demonstrator appliance built on a Spartan chassis.

It was not until 2004 before the arrival of the next batch of new appliances with the delivery of two MAN LE12.220 Water Tender Ladders built by Carmichaels. A further four identical appliances were delivered in 2006.

A disastrous fire broke out in one of the appliance bays of the college in May 2009 destroying eleven fire engines at a total cost of £1,276,000. To allow training to continue the College obtained a number of reserve appliances from brigades including three Volvo FL6.14 Water Tender Ladders from East Sussex and nine similar appliances from Oxfordshire. Also a second-hand Fire Safety Demonstration Unit was obtained from East Sussex Fire and Rescue Service. Built by Baileys on a Volvo FL6 chassis it was converted into an Incident Command Unit.

2006 MAN LE12.220 Water Tender Ladder reg. no. VX56 MHU (photo - The Author)

The College's current Incident Command Unit is this 1999 Volvo FL6 built by Baileys (photo - The Author)

In April 2011 the Government announced it was studying different options for private investment in the College to allow it to achieve its full potential and in March 2012 it was concluded that the best option was full privatisation. In December 2012 Capita was selected as the preferred bidder and the sale was completed for £10 million in early 2013.

The Fire Service College, commonly known as the 'College of Knowledge', provides the full range of training for firefighters at all levels, including initial training for recruit firefighters and operational training is carried out in several purpose built areas of the college, which include:-

- A breathing apparatus complex
- Industrial complexes
- A domestic property
- A high rise building
- Areas for electrical, pool fires and fixed installation training
- Small-scale versions of petroleum and chemical installations
- A concrete ship "Sir Henry"
- A railway, which includes a section of rail with locomotives and carriages of various types, both passenger and freight
- A mock motorway (M96)
- Areas for USAR (Urban Search and Rescue) training
- A range of aircraft including helicopters, military and civil passenger aircraft
- Fire behaviour units

To support the operational training the College has a fully equipped appliance room with large workshops to maintain the appliances and all the other operational equipment.

CHAPTER 9
NATIONAL RESILIENCE APPLIANCES

The National Resilience programme was set up following the disastrous events in New York on the 11th September 2001. The intention was to ensure that the UK's Fire and Rescue Services could cope with any major chemical, nuclear, biological and terrorist threat. The programme was established by the Office of the Deputy Prime Minister (ODPM) to ensure that the Fire and Rescue Services are equipped and trained to deal with not only the aforementioned threats but also serious flooding, building collapses and natural disasters. The ODPM was succeeded by the Fire and Resilience Directorate (FRD) which is part of the Department for Communities and Local Government. Originally all vehicles and equipment remained the property of the FRD but since 2009 ownership has passed to the local Fire and Rescue Services.

Since first being set up the equipment has been used on a number of times for large scale flooding incidents and building collapses as well as being used for local incidents.

Incident Response Units

The first part of the programme was the development and supply of mass decontamination vehicles, known as Incident Response Units (IRUs). Each IRU carries two MD1 decontamination units, each capable of treating two hundred casualties an hour. Supporting equipment carried includes detergent, disrobe and re-robe packs, pumps, water heaters, lighting, gas-tight suits and detection and monitoring equipment. The decontamination units are tent-like structures fourteen metres long and comprises three sections for disrobing, showering and re-robing. One smaller

MAN TG-A 6x2 Incident Response Unit built by Marshall SV of
Cambridge and a Moffett Mounty Forklift Truck
(The Author's Collection)

MD4 decontamination unit is also carried to enable decontamination of firefighters at the scene. The equipment is carried in twelve container pallets stacked two high and unloaded by a Moffett Mounty M2003E forklift truck which is carried on the rear of the appliance. The vehicles were built by Marshall SV of Cambridge on the MAN TG-A 26.363 6x2 chassis

Prime Movers

Following the successful delivery of the IRUs, Marshall SV was awarded the contract for the supply of the fleet of Prime Movers. The vehicles are again built on the MAN TG-A 26.363 chassis but this time on a 6x4 configuration with air suspension on the rear and leaf suspension on the front. The units are shorter than the IRUs and were given the 6x4 configuration for better traction control.

The system for loading and unloading the pod units is a Partec Multilift LHS 260.51 hook-lift installation with a lifting capacity of twenty tonnes. The Prime Movers were designed to carry a variety of demountable pods including High Volume Pumping Units, Urban Search and Rescue Units and Mass Decontamination Disrobe and Re-Robe Units.

A MAN TG-A 6x4 Prime Mover again built by Marshall SV of Cambridge seen here unloading a pod. The Multilift equipment can clearly be seen (photo – Mike Sudds)

High Volume Pumping Units

The High Volume Pumping Units (HVPUs) were supplied by Kuiken Hytrans of Holland and each set consists of:-

- One Pump Unit consisting of a diesel-hydraulic power unit and a portable floating submersible pump.
- Three Hose Boxes each containing one kilometre of 152mm hose.
- Two Hose Recovery Units.
- Two containers with double Equipment Cabinets.

A Prime Mover carries a Pod fitted with a double Equipment Cabinet at the front end with compartments for portable equipment and a Hose Recovery Unit which allows recovery from either side. Behind the cabinets are loaded either (a) a Pump Unit and one Hose Box or (b) two Hose Boxes.

A Kuiken Hytrans High Volume Pumping Unit seen mounted on a Prime Mover (photo – Gary Chapman)

Urban Search and Rescue Units

Each complete Urban Search and Rescue Unit (USAR) consists of five pods of various types. The contract for the supply of the pod units was awarded to John Dennis Coachbuilders (JDC) who adapted and fitted out containers supplied by Bootle Containers Ltd. Externally Pods 1, 2 and 3 are identical.

- Pod 1 carries equipment for scene safety, technical search, electric generators, lighting, timber and concrete cutting and drilling.
- Pod 2 contains heavy cutting, heavy lifting and confined space and rope access equipment for use in major transport incidents including rail and aircraft.
- Pod 3 was developed to support Pod 1 at structural collapses and includes timber supports, heavy breaking and breaching tools, heavy lifting equipment, access platforms and lighting.
- Pod 4 is a drop-side unit and carries a logistics and servicing structure and a Bobcat 4-wheel drive multi-purpose vehicle capable of transporting equipment to an incident site and moving rubble to clear sites.
- Pod 5 is a flat-bed unit which carries ten tonnes of pre-cut timber for shoring unstable structures.

Mass Decontamination Disrobe and Re-Robe Units

The Mass Decontamination Disrobe (MDD) and Re-Robe (MDR) Units are externally identical to the USAR pods with the exception of not having side access doors and are designed to replenish the IRUs with consumables as decontamination progresses. The units were again supplied by Bootle Containers Ltd. and fitted out by JDC. The MDD contains 1,600 disrobe packs and one MD4 decontamination shower structure. The MDR contains 1,500 re-robe packs for use by decontaminated casualties and one MD4 decontamination shower structure.

A MAN TG-A Prime Mover seen with an Urban Search and Rescue Pod mounted on it (photo – Gary Chapman)

Urban Search and Rescue Unit Pod 1. Seen here with the access doors open, the method of stowage can clearly be seen (photo – Mike Sudds)

Urban Search and Rescue Unit Pod 4 seen here loaded on a Prime Mover (photo – Mike Sudds)

Bobcat 4-wheel drive Multi-Purpose Vehicle which is carried on
Pod 4 of the Urban Search and Rescue Unit
(photo – Mike Sudds)

Urban Search and Rescue Unit Pod 5 seen here loaded on a Prime
Mover (photo – Mike Sudds)

This Prime Mover is seen loaded with a Mass Decontamination
Disrobe Pod (photo – Gary Chapman)

Detection, Identification and Monitoring Units

The Detection, Identification and Monitoring Units (DIM) are based on white Iveco Daily 50C17 extra high roof vans divided into three sections; the front section is a three-person crew cab, the middle section has been built to form an office area provided with communications equipment and a computer for analysing sample information. The rear of the vehicle forms a storage area for gas-tight suits, breathing apparatus, one MD4 decontamination shower structure and scene lighting.   Equipment carried includes an infrared spectroscope, radiation survey meters, gas detectors and instruments for chemical, vapour and isotope identification.   Communication systems, satellite telephones and data transfer equipment are also carried. Gas-tight suits and breathing apparatus are provided for the crew.

An Iveco Daily 50C17 Detection, Identification and Monitoring Unit
(The Author's Collection)

APPENDIX

Dennis Bros., Leyland Motors and Merryweather & Sons were names associated with the manufacturer of fire appliances long before the First World War and built the majority of British fire appliances between the two World Wars. Following the end of the Second World War they soon re-entered the market. Many other companies also entered into competition both with a variety of chassis types but there were even larger number of bodywork companies, some of which only lasted a few years, others are still in production even if the ownership of the company has changed.

Appliance Manufacturers

AEC. A manufacturer of commercial chassis which began to produce a fire engine chassis before the Second World War. Following the end of the war the AEC Regal, Regent and Mercury chassis were used to produce a whole variety of fire engines, the best known being the Mercury chassis fitted with a Merryweather Turntable Ladder. The company became part of Leyland in 1962 and by the early 1970s the name of AEC had disappeared.

Albion Motors. A manufacturer of commercial vehicles based in Bathgate, Scotland. The company became part of Leyland in 1951 and by 1980 the name of Albion was dropped.

Angloco. Originally named Anglo Coachbuilders, Angloco is an independent company, based in Batley, West Yorkshire, which has been designing and building fire fighting and rescue vehicles for over 45 years. Angloco build on various commercial chassis and their appliances range from Water Tenders through to high-rise Aerial Ladder Platforms.

Austin. A long established vehicle manufacturer, Austin entered the fire engine market in 1939 building large numbers of government utility appliances. They utilised the K2 chassis cab for Auxiliary Towing Vehicles and the larger K4 model for both Heavy Units and hand operated 60ft. Turntable Ladders. Many of these wartime appliances were taken over by the post-war brigades and some were still on the run into the 1960s.

Bedford. Prior to World War II Bedford built a number of pumping appliances but after the war the Bedford chassis was used for both pumping appliances and special appliances. In the early 1950s the S and SB models were very popular and when a new vehicle was required for the Auxiliary Fire Service in 1953 Bedford was the preferred chassis supplier and hundreds of the 'Green Goddesses' were built. During the 1960s and 1970s a wide range of Bedford chassis became available including the TJ, TK, TKL, TKEL and TKGS and were used for a variety of fire appliance applications. In 1988 Bedford ceased production of commercial chassis but many Bedford fire engines are still in use around the world.

W.H. Bence. The company is a specialist coachbuilder formed in 1982 using the former premises of Longwell Green Coachworks in Yate just outside Bristol.

A.G. Bracey. The company was formed in 1962 by a former apprentice of Longwell Green Coachworks at some old farm buildings on the outskirts of Bristol. The initial core business was the repair of accident damaged light vehicles but a change of direction in the early 1970s took the company into the manufacture of commercial vehicle bodywork. The company expanded in 1980 and opened new headquarters at Pucklechurch, Bristol.

Carmichael & Sons. The company's origins go back to the 19th century but it was not until 1950 that they built their first fire appliance. One of the 'big 4' of UK manufacturers its vehicles have been supplied worldwide. In 1992 the Carmichael Group of companies faced financial difficulties and the group went into administrative receivership. The receivers agreed a deal with Trinity Holdings and under their ownership Carmichaels continued to supply vehicles both to the UK and overseas. Currently the company is known as Amdac Carmichael Ltd.

Cheshire Fire Engineering (CFE). Based in Sandbach, Cheshire the company was formed by a management buyout of the bodywork side of ERF. CFE closed down in 1982.

Commer. In the early post-war years the QX chassis was very popular for use as a Water Tender. The introduction of other chassis's allowed for the building of Turntable Ladders and Hydraulic Platforms. Commer ceased production of a chassis suitable for use as fire engines in 1975.

Dennis Bros. Established in 1901 by two brothers John & Raymond they built their first fire engine at their workshops in Guildford, Surrey, in 1908. Another of the 'big 4' of suppliers to fire brigades. The F series was introduced after World War II and continued to be built into the 1970s. The 1960s had seen the introduction of the D series and then in 1976 the R series was introduced. In 1972 the company had been bought by Hestair and renamed Hestair Dennis. By 1979 the R series was phased out in favour of the RS model and SS tilt cab version. A decision was made in 1983 to concentrate on chassis production only and to leave the bodywork side to specialist companies and in 1985 the company was renamed Dennis Specialist Vehicles. The Rapier chassis was launched in 1991 followed by the Sabre in 1994 and later the Dagger but production of a fire appliance chassis ceased in 2007.

John Dennis Coachbuilders Ltd. John Dennis, grandson of one of the original founders of Dennis Brothers, started up his own company after Hestair Dennis ceased building bodies onto their chassis. John Dennis Coachbuilders Limited, known as JDC, bodied its first appliance in 1986 on a Dennis chassis followed in 1988 by its first non-Dennis based vehicle.

Dodge. The Dodge chassis was used in the 1950s and 1960s for a small range of pumping appliances but with the introduction, in the 1970s, of the K and G range of chassis Dodge entered the UK market in a big way. The K850 and the K13 series were used for Water Tenders whilst the heavier G16 range was used for Turntable Ladders and Hydraulic Platforms. In the early 1980s Dodge was acquired by Renault and the old badge was soon replaced by the new logo.

Dodge Kew. In the 1920s Dodge Motors in Park Royal, London had been taken over by the Chrysler Corporation. When production was moved to the Chrysler factory in Kew, Surrey, more and more British components were used and vehicles built there became known as Dodge Kew.

Emergency One (UK) Ltd. Based in Cumnock, Scotland, the company built its first fire appliance in 1991 and with a workforce of nearly 100 personnel build approximately 80 fire appliances annually based on various commercial chassis.

Evems Ltd. The company was formed in 2005 at Bawtry near Doncaster to meet a demand for good quality second hand fire appliances for use by industrial brigades and overseas customers. The company now also build rapid response vehicles on various chassis with a variety of body styles.

ERF. Founded by Edwin Richard Foden in Sandbach, Cheshire, the company launched two new chassis in the late 1960s aimed at the fire engine market. The 84RF was designed for Water Tender use and the heavier 84PF was designated for mounting Turntable Ladders and Hydraulic Platforms. ERF ceased fire engine production in 1982 but re-emerged in 1996 when a number of new appliances entered service using the EC8 series chassis.

Excalibur Ltd. From its factory in Burslem, Staffordshire, Excalibur produced its first two firefighting appliances in 1986; a Bedford Water Tender and Land Rover Light Pump. The company grew progressively to become a prominent builder of a full range of fire appliances but went into receivership and ceased trading in August 2004.

Ford. During the Second World War the Auxiliary Fire Service was supplied with large numbers of Heavy Units many based on the Fordson 7V chassis. After de-nationalisation many were absorbed in the newly formed brigades as Pumps whilst others were rebuilt into other roles such as Emergency Tenders, Salvage Tenders etc. In the 1950s the Thames Trader chassis was used to build a number of fire appliances and when the improved D series was launched in 1965 large numbers of Water Tenders were built on the D1014 chassis. The smaller Ford A series and the Ford Transit were used as Rescue Tenders or lightweight fire tenders. In 1986 the commercial vehicle division of Ford was acquired by Iveco.

Fulton & Wylie. Based in Irvine, Scotland this company was formed in 1959 and its first foray into the fire appliance market was in 1967 when they rebuilt two accident damaged appliances for the Western Area Fire Brigade of Scotland. Following this success they soon began building new appliance bodies on varied commercial chassis. The largest single order was for twelve Water Tenders for Greater Manchester Fire Brigade in 1991 followed by ten Volvo based appliances for Suffolk Fire Brigade in 1992 shortly before the company folded.

G & T Fire Control. A company which made its name in the refitting of old turntable ladders and hydraulic platforms onto new chassis at its factory in Gravesend, Kent.

Hampshire Car Bodies. HCB as the company was known commenced by converting ex-National Fire Service vehicles in the late 1940s but soon began to build new appliances. In 1964 the company amalgamated with Angus Fire Armour to become HCB-Angus. Another of the 'big 4', whose vehicles were supplied to many fire brigades. The company went into liquidation in 1994.

Haws & Co. A company based in Sunbury on Thames which specialised in building van bodies trading under the name Hawson. In 1955 they amalgamated with Garner Motors of Birmingham to form Hawson-Garner and moved to Andover, Hampshire.

David Haydon Ltd. A specialist fire engine bodybuilding and engineering company based in Birmingham. They fitted a number of Magirus Turntable Ladders during the late 1950s and early 1960s but also built the bodywork of a number of specialist fire engines, such as the Leyland Firemaster.

Iveco. Iveco became involved in building fire engines after acquiring the German company Magirus-Deutz. Magirus has long been associated with turntable ladders and the Iveco chassis has been widely used as a base for Magirus ladders which continue to appear under the German name.

J.H. Jennings. A body building company based in Sandbach, Cheshire, which was taken over by ERF and became the ERF Body Division.

Karrier Motors Ltd. The company was formed in 1920 and based in Huddersfield but in 1934 was acquired by Rootes Group and production moved to Luton. In 1965 production again moved this time to nearby Dunstable where Commer, Dodge (UK) and Karrier were all brought together.

Land Rover. In 1948 the Rover Motor Co. produced it first 4x4 vehicles and from the earliest days a number of fire brigades purchased Land Rovers to operate as lightweight fire engines. Modern Land Rover fire engines are based on the Defender chassis while the Range Rover model was first adapted in 1972, when in conjunction with Carmichael Ltd. an extra axle was added to give a 6x4 configuration. This enabled a greater payload to be carried including rescue equipment.

Leyland Motors Ltd. The company based in the Lancashire town after which it was named built its first fire engine in 1910. After the end of the Second World War Leyland produced it stylish Comet chassis on which many Water Tenders were built. A major innovation came in 1958 with the introduction of the Firemaster chassis which allowed a pump and its controls to be fitted to the front of the fire engine. Despite its technical features it was not a commercial success and only a few went into service. British Leyland as it later became known was acquired by DAF Vehicles in 1987 and is now known as Leyland-DAF.

Longwell Green Ltd. A vehicle body company which was based in a suburb of the same name on the eastern fringe of Bristol.

M.A.N. In the UK the MAN chassis was originally used for special appliances such as Emergency Tenders, Control Units and Prime Movers. In addition a number of Metz Turntable Ladders on the MAN chassis have gone into service. More recently the MAN chassis is being used for Water Tenders.

Marshall Special Vehicles. Marshall SV, part of the Marshall Group of Cambridge, was formed in 1948 to build bodies on commercial chassis's and specialised vehicles for the Ministry of Defence etc. Following the disastrous events in New York on the 11th September 2001 the British government instigated a program to build of fleet of vehicles for the Fire and Rescue Services to use for protection against terrorist attacks and natural disasters. Marshall SV won the contract to provide 80 Incident Response Units and 238 Prime Mover all to be built on the MAN TG-A 26.363 chassis.

Mercedes-Benz. With its headquarters in Stuttgart, Germany, the company is one of the largest manufacturers of commercial trucks. The range of chassis available for fire service use includes the Unimog 4x4 all-terrain vehicle, the 1124AF for Water Tenders, the 1625, 1726 and 1827 series as bases for Turntable Ladders and Aerial Ladder Platforms. The latest Atego series is in use for Water Tenders and Rescue Vehicles.

Merryweather & Sons Ltd. For over a century Merryweather was one of the biggest names in fire engines. The company built its first steam-powered pump in 1861. The first petrol engined appliance was built in 1903 followed by the first Turntable Ladder in 1908. Merryweather continued to build Turntable Ladders and other appliances, usually on the various AEC chassis. The last of the 'big 4' its vehicles were supplied worldwide. Originally based at its factory in Greenwich, London, Merryweather were taken over by Siebe Gorman and moved the factory to South Wales. However after a sudden move to Plymouth this long standing manufacturer was closed down in 1984.

Alfred Miles & Co. Based in Cheltenham the company pioneered the use of light alloys in aircraft assembly and then in the 1950s broke into the fire engine market building bodies onto both Bedford and Commer chassis. These were a new design incorporating high visibility windscreens, folding access doors and roller shutters. In the early 1960s the company was taken over by Dennis Bros. and for a short period continued with the same style of bodywork then known as the Dennis M series.

Mountain Range Ltd. Named after its owner Ron Mountain the company had been converting commercial vehicles into fire appliances, at its factory in Crewe, Cheshire, for the export market. A new factory was opened in 1982 to cope with increasing orders for the UK market. In 1991 the original company ceased trading and a new company Reliance Mercury was formed but eventually that too stopped producing fire appliances.

Mumford Ltd. A coach building company based in Plymouth. They built a number of fire appliances for fire brigades in the South West during the 1950s mainly on the Bedford chassis.

Oldland Motor Body Builders. Oldlands were based at Victoria Works, Oldland Common on the eastern outskirts of Bristol. They built a number of appliances on the Bedford chassis in the 1950s followed by two more in the 1970s.

PolyBilt. PolyBilt is a manufacturer of one piece copolymer bodies built for the fire and rescue industry complete with integrated water tanks.

Saxon Specialist Vehicles. Saxon SV was founded by former Cheshire Fire Engineering staff when CFE closed down in 1982. Two years later the company became known as Saxon Sanbec. The company was renamed Saxon Specialist Vehicles in 2002 but just before Christmas 2004 Saxon SV suddenly announced that it was to cease trading.

Scania. Originally trading in Sweden as Scania-Vagis it merged in 1969 with Saab to become Saab-Scania although the truck division trades as simply Scania. The first Scania fire engines in the UK were Turntable Ladders built in the early 1980s but were soon followed by Water Tenders built on the G92M chassis. The current range includes Water Tenders built on the P94 chassis and a 4x4 version on the P124 model. Many modern Scania chassis are also in use as Emergency or Rescue Tenders, Foam Tenders and Prime Movers. The P124 chassis is also available in a 6x4 version available for a range of Turntable Ladders and Aerial Ladder Platforms.

Shelvoke and Drewry. Based in Letchworth, Hertfordshire, the company was originally a builder of municipal vehicles but in the 1970s turned its attention to the fire service market. Up to 1986 the company built Water Tenders and Turntable Ladders as well as a number of special appliances using the WX and WY chassis but now only a few vehicles survive in preservation.

TVAC. The Vehicle Applications Centre, more commonly known as TVAC, was based in Leyland, Lancashire and began building fire appliances in 1996. A bodywork company which although concentrating on building Water Tenders using the Plastisol crew cabs and bodies also manufactured other 'special' appliances. TVAC entered administration in December 2008 and was wound up early the following year.

Volvo. Built in Gothenburg, Sweden it was not until the mid 1980s that Volvo fire engines started to appear in the UK based on the FL6 chassis. Today, Volvo fire engines are in use in many of the UK's fire brigades.

James Whitson Ltd. A company based in West Drayton, Middlesex, which specialised in building buses and coaches but also built fire appliances for a short period in the early 1950s.

Windovers Ltd. From Hendon, Middlesex this company built a number of Leyland Comet appliances in the 1950s.

GLOSSARY

APPLIANCES

Aerial Ladder Platform (ALP). A combined ladder and hydraulic platform appliance fitted with a hinged boom, of 3 sections, capable of rotating around 360 degrees, with a cage and monitor at the top.

Breathing Apparatus Tender (BAT). An appliance which carries a supply of breathing apparatus cylinders and supporting equipment. Some are also fitted with compressors to allow the recharging of cylinders.

Brigade Response Vehicle (BRV). A light vehicle which can deal with small fires such as car fires, chimney fires and grass fires etc. Fitted with a water tank and a pump it carries breathing apparatus, ladders and range of firefighting equipment and can be used in areas of difficult access.

Chemical Incident Unit (CIU). An appliance carrying protective suits and specialist equipment to deal with chemical and other hazardous incidents.

Command Support Unit (CSU). A modern version of a Control Unit invariably fitted with satellite communication equipment.

Control Unit (CU). A mobile control room containing radios, maps etc. used by senior officers to control larger incidents.

Damage Control Unit (DCU). An appliance which carries a variety of equipment to protect property and belongings from damage by water, heat and smoke.

Emergency Tender (ET). A special appliance carrying a large variety of tools and rescue equipment, basically a mobile workshop.

Escape Carrying Unit (ECU). A wartime appliance which carried a 50 feet wheeled escape but without a built in pump but invariably towing a trailer pump. Later many of these were fitted with front mounted Barton pumps and then became Pump Escapes.

Fireboat (FBt). A specialised watercraft with built in fire pumps and deck monitors designed for fighting shipboard and waterside fires.

Hazardous Materials Unit (HMU). See Chemical Incident Unit

Heavy Unit (HU). An appliance supplied as a wartime measure built on a commercial chassis with either a 700 or 1,000 gallons per minute pump mounted on the rear chassis of the vehicle. The pump was powered by a separate engine from the road engine.

Hose Layer (HL). An appliance which carries large diameter hose pre-connected ready to be laid out while the appliance drives from a water source to the fireground.

Hydraulic Platform (HP). An appliance fitted with a hinged boom, of 2 or 3 sections, capable of rotating around 360 degrees, with a cage and monitor at the top.

Incident Control Unit (ICU). See Control Unit.

Operational Support Unit (OSU). An appliance which carries out a variety of roles dependent on local requirements.

Pod. Container type unit built to be loaded onto a Prime Mover.

Prime Mover (PM). An appliance consisting of a crew cab and an open chassis onto which a variety of pods can be loaded and unloaded at incidents.

Pump (P). A pumping appliance which carries a 30 feet ladder but with a limited water capacity. Also a generic term for any fire appliance carrying a crew of between 4-6, breathing apparatus, ladders and other firefighting and rescue gear and capable of pumping water.

Pump Escape (PE). Similar to a Pump but carried a 50 feet wheeled escape. The last wheeled escape ladder went out of service in the UK in 1994.

Rapid Intervention Unit (RIU). A light vehicle built to provide a quick response to an incident.

Rescue Boat (RBt). There are two types of Rescue Boat in use with the fire and rescue services. (a) A lightweight, high performance boat constructed with a solid hull and inflated flexible tubes at the gunwales. Powered by an outboard motor they are generally towed on trailers. (b) An inflatable boat stowed in a folded state on an appliance which can be quickly inflated using air cylinders and powered by an outboard engine.

Rescue Pump (RP). A Water Tender Ladder with enhanced rescue capabilities.

Rescue Tender (RT) or Rescue Vehicle (RV). A special appliance carrying tools and rescue equipment.

Salvage Tender. See Damage Control Unit.

Special Appliance. Any non-pumping fire engine e.g. Turntable Ladder, Rescue Tender etc.

Turntable Ladder (TL). An appliance fitted with an extending ladder capable of rotating around 360 degrees. Normally the ladders are 100 feet but wartime variants were built with 60 feet ladders.

Trailer Pump (TrP). Pumps mainly used during the Second World War carried on a two wheeled trailer and towed behind a variety of vehicles.

Water Carrier (WrC). An appliance built specifically to carry a large quantity of water.

Water/Foam Carrier (WFoU). Similar to a Water Carrier but carries foam as well as water.

Water Tender (WrT). A pumping appliance which carries a 35 feet extension ladder and is fitted with a 1,800 litres (400 gallons) water tank.

Water Tender Escape (WrE). Same as a Water Tender but carrying a 50 feet wheeled escape ladder. It has now been superseded by the Water Tender Ladder.

Water Tender Ladder (WrL). Same as a Water Tender but carries a 45 feet extension ladder.

SPECIAL NOTES (Water Tenders)
War-time. A converted lorry with either a canvas dam with a steel frame or a galvanised iron tank fitted to the lorry bed. A hosereel was fitted together with a light pump. The unit invariably towed a trailer pump.

Type A. A purpose built appliance developed from the above, carrying 400 gallons of water, two 180 ft. hosereels and carrying a light detachable pump. A trailer pump was also towed.

Type B (from 1955). As above but fitted with a main pump driven via the road engine and carrying a light portable pump.

DUTY SYSTEMS
Wholetime. A system which maintains 24 hour cover on fire stations. Although there are varying systems in operation the standard UK system involves four watches (Red, White, Blue and Green). One watch works a day shift; one works a night shift with the other two watches off duty. The system covers an eight day period; two day shifts, two night shifts and four days off duty.

Day Crewed. A system which uses full-time firefighters who crew the appliance(s) during the daytime but respond to alerter callout from their homes close to the fire station at night.

Retained. A system used in smaller towns or villages where the crew is made up of on-call firefighters who follow their normal jobs and respond from work or home in response to an alerter call. They are paid fees to cover the time they spend on duty.

Volunteer. Stations where call numbers are very low e.g. Lundy Island in the Bristol Channel where the crew is made up of on-call firefighters who receive no remuneration for their work.